Acclaim for *Remain in Me and I in You*

"Who doesn't yearn to know, love and serve God more perfectly? In *Remain in Me and I in You,* Fr. Wayne Sattler provides a helpful guide for encountering the God who yearns to be known by each of us. A keen observer of the human experience and a devoted student of the Carmelite masters, Fr. Sattler distills and shares what he has learned about how we can enter a personal relationship with our loving God. Drawing on his rich experiences as a hermit and shepherd of souls, as well as on the wisdom of some of the greatest witnesses to the Faith in the modern age (especially St. Teresa of Calcutta, Pope St. John Paul II, and Pope Benedict XVI), Fr. Sattler has given us a gem that is both inspiring and practical."

—Archbishop Bernard A. Hebda,
Archdiocese of St. Paul and Minneapolis

"*Remain in Me and I in You* follows upon Fr. Sattler's first work and complements it in a very powerful yet practical way. This book takes the reader to the heart of prayer—knowing, loving, and serving God as an intimate friend. Best of all, Fr. Sattler shows us that God is the One who draws us into this intimate and best friendship. I recommend this book to anyone seeking a deeper life of prayer. It is a manual both on how to pray and why we must pray."

—Bishop David D. Kagan, Diocese of Bismarck

"Fr. Sattler once again delves into the depths of the spiritual life in a very accessible manner. This book reminds us that prayer is truly a love story and a relationship between us and God. Readers will be reinvigorated in their desires for a life of prayer, which is the most exciting journey of a lifetime."

—Bishop David L. Toups, Diocese of Beaumont

"This is a work of remarkable contemplative depth, but one of its most engaging features is its conversational directness and simplicity. Fr. Wayne speaks to us as much from the heart as from the head. His focus throughout is on the three most important things in the spiritual life: knowing God, loving God, and serving God. This is not an academic text. It is a luminous book to be prayed with and lived with."

—*Fr. Paul Murray, O.P.,* Professor Emeritus, The Angelicum

Remain in Me and I in You

FATHER WAYNE SATTLER

REMAIN in ME and I in YOU

RELATING TO GOD AS A PERSON, NOT AN IDEA

SOPHIA INSTITUTE PRESS
Manchester, New Hampshire

*Special thanks to Joanie Agamenoni
for her initial read-through of this text,
and to Deacon David Fleck, Dr. Elizabeth Jones
and Sara Keller for their willingness to consult
and eagerness to encourage*

CONTENTS

Remain in Me and I in You

Is God a Person or an Idea to You?

I will always remember the first time I heard that question come out of my mouth. It is a question I have come to ask many times since. It was first raised during a retreat I was giving for a group of consecrated religious sisters. At the time I was living as a diocesan hermit in a one-room cabin in rural North Dakota.

In the six years I was graced to follow that contemplative vocation, I was allowed to go out two times a year to give retreats for priests and consecrated religious communities. The retreats would be either five or eight days long. Days of retreats would consist of giving two talks, each one an hour in length, and meeting individually with the retreatants as requested. During a retreat for a group of consecrated religious sisters preparing to make their final vows, I was asked to meet daily with one of the sisters.

Within this particular community, prior to making their final vows, a sister would have typically already been with them for ten years to receive proper formation and to allow a thorough discernment to be made as to whether God was calling her to remain in this vocation. The superior who asked me to meet with this sister was careful to note how she had a way of truly standing out in the very difficult work of their mission. She was an authentically beautiful person, exteriorly and interiorly, and a highly intellectual woman who had held a position of prominence in the world prior to converting to the Catholic Faith and then entering religious life.

The sister, however, was questioning making her final vows. She confided how the past summer she was particularly drawn to the priest in the parish they were assisting. She was grateful that nothing physical had unfolded between them, but her heart was troubled. She remarked, "Father, he wasn't even that great. What happens when Mr. Wonderful comes into the room?"

I paused, looked her in the eye, and responded, "Sister, if Mr. Wonderful has not already entered the room, we have a problem." It immediately struck me that it might be good to clarify that I was not referring to myself. In that humbling moment, the way was cleared for the Lord to place these words into my heart for the first time, as I asked, "Sister, is God a person or an idea to you?"

The question caught us both off guard, a telling sign that it was coming from the Lord. He had a purpose for this question to be asked in that moment, and in every moment it has since been asked. In this moment, the sister was a bit stunned by the question. She bowed her head in a long, uncomfortable silence. It was a silence I did not dare to interrupt. Finally she slowly raised her head, and I will always recall the distinct sadness in her eyes as she responded, "It seems, Father, that He is more of an idea than a person."

When God seems to be more of an idea than a person, there will be a distinct sadness. It was the same sadness seen clearly on the face of the rich young man we encounter in the Gospel, to whom Jesus said, "If you wish to be perfect, go, sell what you have and give to the poor, and you will have treasure in heaven. Then come, follow me," for "when the young man heard this statement, he went away sad, for he had many possessions" (Matt. 19:21–22).

It can be helpful to place these two souls side by side. For today some might be tempted to contend that the reason it is hard to know Jesus as a person is because Jesus has ascended into heaven. We do not hear and see Jesus as we do other people. If only Jesus were standing before me right now as you are, it would be much easier.

I am not so sure about that.

Standing right in front of the rich young man was Jesus. The rich young man, like this religious sister, was no spiritual slouch. He had faithfully kept all the commandments since his youth. He was drawn to Jesus, ran up to Jesus, knelt down before Jesus, and asked, "Good teacher, what good must I do to inherit eternal life?" (Mark 10:17). What he didn't realize was that eternal life was standing right there in front of him!

Mr. Wonderful had entered the room!

Had the rich young man been living in the United States between 1885 and the 1960s, he would have faithfully memorized the answers to questions posed in the *Baltimore Catechism.* This was the standard Catholic school text that was used to help form us, like the rich young man, to faithfully keep the commandments from our youth. The *Baltimore Catechism* begins with the important first question, "*Who made us?*" By memorizing the answer to that question, we could remember that "God made us."

The third question, "*Why did God make us?*" would keep fresh in our minds how "God made us to show forth His goodness and to share with us His everlasting happiness in heaven."

The very key fourth question, "*What must we do to gain the happiness of heaven?*" is very similar to the question asked by the rich young man: "Good teacher, what good must I do to inherit eternal life?" The answer is one we all hope to take to heart: "To gain the happiness of heaven, we must know, love and serve God in this world."

Unfortunately, it is possible to know all the right answers, to faithfully keep all the commandments, to stand out in the very difficult work of the Church, and yet still not know God, love God, or serve God.

As the foundress of the Missionaries of Charity, St. Teresa of Calcutta (Mother Teresa) would wisely ask her sisters a very telling question, "Do you really know the living Jesus, not through books, but by being with Him in your heart?"

What the rich young man knew of eternal life might have been from what he read in books. Eternal life for him was an idea in his head, something to be obtained by doing certain necessary things, just as there were things he needed to do to gain his many other possessions. The rich young man was diligently trying to check off the right boxes to inherit eternal life. Eternal life, however, is not an idea. "Eternal life," Jesus tells us in the Gospel of John, is this: "that they should know you, the only true God, and the one whom you sent, Jesus Christ" (17:3). Eternal life is a person. In fact, it is three Persons! Eternal life is the relationship we have now and forever with the Father and the Son and the Holy Spirit.

What is quite beautiful is how Eternal Life, in Person, turns to pursue the rich young man. Jesus looks at the rich young man, loves the rich young man, and observes of this rich young man, "You are lacking in one thing" (Mark 10:21). The one thing he was lacking was a relationship with Jesus!

Now, imagine if someone was to approach you to tell you that you were lacking in one thing, referring to themselves, and invite you to follow them—without even knowing where they were going? Even if that person was particularly charismatic or attractive, would you drop everything to follow them? Probably not—especially considering how the prophet Isaiah foretold of Jesus that there would be "in him no stately bearing to make us look at him, nor appearance that would attract us to him" (Isa. 53:2).

It is all the more striking, then, to consider what happened to Peter, Andrew, James, John, and Matthew when Jesus came and stood before them. He went in pursuit of them to their places of work, looked at them, loved them, and invited them to "follow me." They dropped everything—their nets, the money they were counting—and followed Him. In their heart the connection was made; they were able to recognize Jesus as the one thing they were lacking.

Jesus pursues the rich young man with a very similar invitation, "Go, sell what you have … then come, follow me" (Mark 10:21). Unfortunately, the connection in his heart was not made. He did not recognize Jesus as the one thing he was lacking. "At that statement his face fell, and he went away sad, for he had many possessions" (Mark 10:22). Eternal life would remain for him an idea to pursue for the future, while the relationship with Eternal Life, in Person, was standing right there before him.

The world seems to be filled with souls whose knowledge about eternal life comes from what they read in books. They can seem to be sad, burdened with needing to go through the motions they hear are needed to enter eternal life: going to Mass, going to Confession, even finding time to pray. Their hearts do not seem to be making the connection with God as the one thing they are lacking!

At the same time, there are souls who are clearly recognizing a voice in their hearts inviting them to "follow me," who appreciate Him as the one thing they are lacking: the "pearl of great price" (Matt. 13:46); the treasure, which "out of joy" one "goes and sells all they have" to obtain (Matt. 13:44).

When we engage others with only our mind, we treat them as more of an idea than the person that each one is. To relate to anyone as the person they are, our heart needs to be engaged. It is the same thing in our relationship with God. When God is engaged with only the mind but not the heart, He is treated more like an idea. To relate to God as the person He is—in fact, the three Persons He has revealed Himself to be—the heart must be engaged. Only then do we appreciate God as the person we can know, the person we can love, the person we can serve.

No matter how advanced we may become in our relationship with the Father and the Son and the Holy Spirit, there will remain moments when we all lapse into treating God more as an idea than a person. It is important to follow up on the wise counsel of the *Baltimore Catechism* in continuing to strive "to know, love, and serve God in this world." What will follow in this book are reflections on those three themes: *Knowing God, Loving God,* and *Serving God.*

I realize it may seem a bit ironic to encourage others to read on in a book that begins with a challenge to not base their knowledge of Jesus on what they read in books. To be honest, it had never been my intention to become an author. This book, just as my first, *And You Will Find Rest: What God Does in Prayer*, is based on the material I would use for retreats, classes, and parish missions. When people began asking me for the notes, these books became the fruit of that prompting.

In my own journey with the Lord in my heart, I am grateful for the authentic companions the Lord has allowed to accompany me, some through what they have written. I am grateful that *And You Will Find Rest* has helped others in their journey with the Lord in their heart, and I am hopeful that this book will serve a similar purpose: that it might in some way accompany you on the journey in your own heart to so know God, love God, and serve God that you *Remain in Me and I in You.*

KNOWING GOD

Every person, human or divine, is a mystery hidden from others. To know any person, they must first choose to reveal themself. What a person reveals about who they are is then either believed or not believed.

For example, I sometimes choose to reveal that I met Mother Teresa, that through a few graced encounters an endearing connection was made. These encounters unfolded while I was a seminarian studying in Rome during the years she was alive. I volunteered regularly at a homeless shelter run by her sisters, and when Mother would come periodically to visit them, the sisters were kind enough to open an opportunity for me to spend some time with her during those visits. I now hold as dear mementos a few pictures of us together, as well as some items she gave me, a few with her signature.

We all know, however, that the information people choose to reveal is not always true. Today, perhaps more than ever, we are confronted by the reality that there is much false information out there, even photographs are faked and signatures forged. In the end, you would either believe me or not believe me.

The same is true of God. What is revealed to us about the Second Person of the Blessed Trinity is so wonderful, so unique, so accurately described by St. Paul as "what eye has not seen, and ear has not heard, and what has not entered the human heart" (1 Cor. 2:9).

Jesus revealed that He has come down from Heaven (John 6:38). He revealed that the God who created the universe is Our Father, Abba, Daddy (Matt. 6:9). He claimed that He and the Father are one (John 10:30). He prayed that the love between the Father and Him would be in us (John 17:26). He promised to send the Paraclete upon us, so that this love between Them might be in us and we might do His works and even greater (John 14:12). Can this all possibly be true? Can the one true God really be the three persons of the Father and the Son and the Holy Spirit that Jesus revealed God to be, or is what Jesus revealed a very nice, but unbelievable, idea?

To sincerely believe what a person reveals about who they are is fundamental to a relationship. Without this belief, there can be no real intimacy. To "believe in the one he sent," Jesus says, "this is the work of God" (John 6:29). It was only recently that I ran across a reflection on the priesthood by Benedict XVI in which he stated that "the first 'task' a priest has to do is to be a believer."[1]

In all my years of being a priest, I have never heard it put that simply. To be honest, this came as a relief. I

---

[1] Benedict XVI (Joseph Cardinal Ratzinger), *A New Song for the Lord: Faith in Christ and Liturgy Today* (New York: Crossroad, 1996), p. 47.

am blessed to be surrounded by many holy, dynamic, and charismatic priests. Comparing myself to them, there are many things I am not. Yet, by God's grace, I am a believer.

When I was preparing to enter the hermitage, many questioned the wisdom of this young priest going out there alone to do nothing. I was thirty-seven years old at the time and had been ordained a priest for nine years. I remember going to Abbot Brian Wangler at Assumption Abbey in Richardton, North Dakota, for some direction on all of this. Abbot Wangler was not a stern-looking, fist-slamming type of man. He was a very gentle, humble, and unassuming soul. So it has remained engraved upon my memory when he took me into his office, looked at me sternly, and said, "Wayne, may your entrance into the hermitage help people to realize that God is as real as the wood of this desk," as he slammed his fist into the desk.

This really stirred his passion. Living within the great monastic tradition, he was aware of the truth recognized among the saints that "the man who has God with him is never less alone than when he is alone."[2]

A truth that was perhaps first coined by Cicero, who even before the coming of Christ remarked, "I am never less alone than when I am alone."

---

[2] William of St. Thierry, *The Golden Epistle*, trans. Theodore Berkeley, O.C.S.O. (Kalamazoo, MI: Cistercian Publications, 1980), p. 19.

Being left alone can also be used as a form of torture. Solitary confinement is when they put you in a cell all by yourself as a severe punishment. Being left alone with just your thoughts for too long can drive you crazy. You may start talking to yourself.

There is a telling line in the 1972 dark comedy *The Ruling Class* in which actor Peter O'Toole played the character Jack Gurney. Jack was a paranoid schizophrenic British nobleman who thought he was God. When asked how he knew he was God, the revealing answer came, "Simple. When I pray to Him, I find I am talking to myself."

When people hear that I lived as a hermit for six years, they likely assume this is a man who did a lot of talking to himself. To monks, however, their cell is not a form of punishment. William of St. Thierry was writing in Latin as he observed for a group of Carthusian monks how "the cell (*cella*) and heaven (*caelum*) are akin to one another:" "when heavenly pursuits are continually practiced in the cell, heaven is brought into close proximity," whereas "the inmates of cells often go down into hell."[3] In their cell, the monk is alone at last with "Him whom my soul loves" (Song 3:3), and "with Him who we know loves us."[4]

---

[3] Ibid., p 20–21. N.B. William of St. Thierry used the medieval spelling of *caelum*, which was *celum*.

[4] St. Teresa of Avila, *The Book of Her Life*, in *The Collected Works of St. Teresa of Avila*, vol. 1, trans. Kieran Kavanaugh, O.C.D., and Otilio Rodriguez, O.C.D. (Washington, D.C.: ICS Publications, 1980), chap. 8, par. 5.

In my six years as a hermit, I came to appreciate the difference between solitude and isolation. Solitude is the conscious choice to be alone with God. Isolation is just being left alone.

Imagine you found yourself suddenly alone in a cell. How much time would pass before you began to wonder how long you were going to be left all alone? Would it take minutes? Hours? Days? Weeks? Or would you feel content, just to be left alone at last with Jesus in your heart?

When I was discerning a possible call to the Carthusians (a religious order of contemplative monks), I spent eight days with them to experience their way of life. On the first day they walked me through the typical daily routine. As they were wrapping up and preparing to leave my cell, I asked when I might be able to go to the chapel to pray. I was told that I would not go to the chapel to pray by myself. We would go there together at the scheduled times; otherwise, I was to remain in my cell. I then asked when I could go outside for a walk. I was told that I would not go outside for a walk by myself. We would go for a three-hour walk together on Sunday; otherwise, I was to remain in my cell. I remember hearing this and feeling more than a bit panicky.

Two of the ways I had come to experience the presence of God most tangibly were in the Eucharist and in nature. Coming up to this remote place in the beautiful setting of the French Arnans Plateau in the Jura

Mountains, and having seen the most prayerful, austere chapel of their charterhouse, I assumed there would be plenty of opportunity to spend time in both places. I had not been prepared to live out the wisdom of the great desert father Abba Moses, who advised the monks under his care to "Go, sit in your cell, and your cell will teach you everything."[5]

The contemplative soul showing me around obviously sensed this panic. He looked at me, loved me, and said, "If you can't find God here [pointing to his heart], you will not find Him anywhere." With that profound statement of his own, he went out of my cell and closed the door.

In that moment, as I sat in my cell, the connection in my heart was being made with the truth this Carthusian monk was trying to help me discover. The same truth Mother Teresa was trying to help her active sisters with in the question we heard earlier: "Do you really know the living Jesus, not through books, but by being with Him in your heart?"

To really know the living Jesus as a person, it is helpful to realize we need only to do with Him what we might do with any person, any person with whom we desire an intimate relationship. Then, since He is God, we eventually do with Him what can only be done with God.

The first step in coming to know any person is to *become aware of their presence.* Imagine as a young man

---

[5] Benedicta Ward, *The Sayings of the Desert Fathers* (Kalamazoo, MI: Cistercian Publications, 1984), p. 139.

Johnny becoming aware of the presence of this "other" across the room. He may admire Susie from a distance, maybe ask around about her. In his mind he may flirt with many ideas about her. However, to know her *as the person she is*, to enter a relationship with *her*, he will need to know her name and then talk to her.

Similarly, through the wonder and beauty of creation, we are drawn to consider the presence of an "*other*" beyond any other. We may ask around about *Him*, have ideas in our mind about *Him*. And yet, to know *Him* as the person He is, to enter into a relationship with *Him* as a person, we will first need to know *His* name and we will need to talk to Him. When we do this with God, we call it prayer.

VOCAL PRAYER

Vocal prayer is first about knowing Whom we are talking to. St. Teresa of Avila warned her sisters that "a prayer in which a person is not aware of whom he is speaking to, what he is asking, who it is who is asking and of whom, I do not call prayer however much the lips move."[6]

"Anyone in the habit of speaking before God's majesty as though he were speaking to a slave," she continued, "without being careful to see how he is

---

[6] St. Teresa of Avila, *The Interior Castle*, in *The Collected Works of St. Teresa of Avila*, vol. 2, trans. Kieran Kavanaugh, O.C.D., and Otilio Rodriguez, O.C.D. (Washington, D.C.: ICS Publications, 1980), dwelling 1, chap. 1, par. 7.

speaking, but saying whatever comes to his head and whatever he has learned from saying at other times, in my opinion is not praying."[7]

When it comes to prayer, far too many souls, even good religious souls, seem to be just moving their lips. There are some who will prove to be talking to themselves. St. Teresa observes how some think they are hearing God speak to them, while in fact they are "gradually composing what they themselves want to be told."[8]

The Sign of the Cross

One of the shortest and most powerful vocal prayers is the Sign of the Cross. In praying the Sign of the Cross, we become aware of how we are now talking to the Father and the Son and the Holy Spirit who have saved us by the wood of the Cross. The Sign of the Cross, perhaps more than any other prayer, can often prove to be a mere moving of lips.

I will always remember being a young first-time pastor of a rural parish. We had just built a new church. One morning prior to daily Mass, I was sitting in the back, praying the Liturgy of Hours. An elderly man came in, put his hand into the baptismal font, looked directly at the crucifix and clearly prayed as he signed himself, "In the name of the Father and of the Son and of the Holy Spirit."

---

[7] Ibid.
[8] Ibid., 6.3.14.

The sight of him praying so devoutly filled me with remorse, for I had just finished a quick gesture over myself while moving my lips with something like "Fathersonholyspirit." God might have wondered whom I was addressing—"Fathersonholyspirit" sounds like just one person.

This elderly soul's devotion, expressed so eloquently through this simple gesture, reminded me that when you want a person's full attention, you look them in the eye and speak their name distinctly. When our parents want our full attention, they look right at us and typically use our full name, middle name included. By contrast, having someone mutter our name while not even looking in our general direction could be interpreted as rudeness.

St. John Chrysostom taught, "Whether or not our prayer is heard depends not on the number of words, but on the fervor of our souls."[9] Is our Sign of the Cross being heard?

The Lord's Prayer

In teaching us to pray, Jesus instructed us to "not be like the hypocrites" (Matt. 6:5). The word *hypocrite* might sound harsh, but in the Greek language in which the New Testament was written, it means an actor. Jesus is warning us not to act as if we have a relationship with God. To

---

[9] St. John Chrysostom, *Ecloga de oratione*, as quoted in *Catechism of the Catholic Church* (St. Paul, MN: The Wanderer Press, 1994), no. 2700.

then help guide us to an authentic relationship with God, the Lord Himself instructs us, "This is how you are to pray" (Matt. 6:9). The very few, powerful words of *The Lord's Prayer* are then revealed to us.

> *Our Father in heaven,*
> *hallowed be your name,*
> *your kingdom come,*
> *your will be done,*
> *on earth as in heaven.*
> *Give us today our daily bread;*
> *and forgive us our debts,*
> *as we forgive our debtors;*
> *and do not subject us to the final test,*
> *but deliver us from the evil one.*
> *(Matt. 6:9–13)*

There was a penitent who had been away from the sacrament of Reconciliation for quite some time. As a penance, I asked them to pray the Lord's Prayer one time. From the other side of the screen, they laughed, "Just one Our Father? That's it?"

"Yes, but *pray* it," I responded. "I could ask you to pray fifty Our Fathers, but then you might just be saying words." These few, powerful words of the Lord's Prayer were a gift from Jesus to His followers, lovingly formed with great care to lead us into a deep relationship with God. Beginning with the first two astounding words — *"Our Father…"* — Jesus utterly transforms the perception we have of God.

Prior to that moment, the name that God had revealed to us was so unlike any other name: "I AM WHO I AM" (Exod. 3:14 RSVCE). This name might have made an intimate relationship with Him seem unlikely. Imagine the delight within Jesus as He revealed to us how God is "Our Father in heaven" (Matt. 6:9). A name we are much more able to relate intimately with as a person, talking to Him as His own dear son or daughter.

As with any person, knowing their name and talking to them is the first important step in relating to them as the person they are. As mentioned earlier, we do with God what we would do with any person, any person with whom we desire an intimate relationship. Then, since He is God, we eventually do with Him what can only be done with God.

The words of the Lord's Prayer are the words of Jesus. They have the power to bring about in us the effect of what they are saying. The first two words enable us to be aware of Whom we are talking to. The petition then made for His name to be hallowed, to be holy, has the power in that moment for His name to be made holy in us. The petition for His kingdom to come has the power for His kingdom to come in us. The petition for His will to be done has the power for His will to be done in us. Our petitions then go on to affirm in us the truth that Our Father in Heaven provides what is daily needed, forgives our sins, delivers us from evil, and we pray leads us not into temptation. What a shame it would be for these words to be a mere movement of our lips, memorized words uttered without fervor.

The Celebration of Holy Mass

How we pray vocally will always be important in our relationship with God. We never get so advanced in prayer that we don't pray vocally. Just as in marriage, a couple is never so intimate that they don't communicate verbally. In an authentic, intimate relationship, the words being spoken are important for both sides to hear.

Take, for instance, our celebration of Holy Mass. The words in the Preface of the Eucharistic Prayer are placed with care to lead us more deeply into what is about to unfold in the relationship between God and His people. The priest begins by saying, "The Lord be with you." The response is given, "And with your spirit."

That response is often given in a manner that could lead you to question if they really mean it. Did that truly express a sincere desire for the Lord to be with my spirit, or was that just acting, a movement of lips with memorized words? It can get worse as the priest continues with the dialogue, "Lift up your hearts." To which the response is given, "We lift them up to the Lord." Those words can be spoken with such a lack of fervor that it would be hard to believe they were bringing about the effect for which they were prayed. How could your hearts be lifted up to the Lord if your voices were hardly raised enough to hear what was being said? Remember: "Whether or not our prayer is heard depends not on the number of words, but on the fervor of our souls."

MEDITATION

In the beginning stages of the human relationship, there is typically great fervor in the desire to communicate verbally as often as possible. This is the natural process through which we come to know the "other" as the person they are. If things continue to progress in the human relationship, we will reflect on these conversations and, at times, to make our thoughts and emotions better known, we will sit down and write them out in a letter. There is nothing quite like receiving a love letter. We enjoy reading love letters again and again and again. How fun is that?

In a similar manner, as our relationship with God progresses, we will want to become better acquainted with His thoughts, His ways, His emotions. In vocal prayer we did all the talking. Meditation is our initial effort to listen to God.

Mental Prayer

Meditation is also referred to as *mental prayer*. Mental prayer, St. Teresa of Avila writes, "is nothing else than a close sharing between friends; it means taking time frequently to be alone with Him who we know loves us."[10]

To know God more distinctly as the person He is, we will need to learn to waste time with God. Of course, the time is not wasted, any more than we would consider it wasted time for a mother to spend all day with her infant. A mother will come to know that little person in a way others will not, because of the amount of time she spends with her infant. When the baby cries, the mother comes to know whether it is a cry of hunger, weariness, or general fussiness. To those who have not spent that kind of time with this infant, the cries can all sound the same. In fact, the cry of this infant might not be distinguishable from the cry of any other infant. A mother knows the cry of her child and from all the time spent together alone with them, she will know what that little person is communicating with each particular cry.

To know God as the person He really is, it requires being alone with Him frequently. Without actual time spent with God, there is a danger that we will never come to know Him as His own person. We might imagine we know what God is thinking, rather than coming to learn over time the subtleties with which He communicates with us. We may presume that God is much angrier than He is, or we could miss how He is grieving over us. We just might utterly fail to grasp His manner

---

[10] St. Teresa of Avila, *The Book of Her Life,* chap. 8, par. 5.

of loving us unless we make the effort that is needed to "be still, and know that I am God!" (Ps. 46:11). To truly know God as the person He is takes time.

Hearing the Word of God

To better acquaint us with His thoughts, His ways, His emotions, God has made the effort to put down in writing the greatest love letter ever written. In Sacred Scripture we hear His thoughts, which are not our thoughts; His ways, which are not our ways (Isa. 55:8). Sacred Scripture helps to make very clear that God is His own person, He has a mind of His own, a will of His own, emotions of His own. Sacred Scripture is the Word of God.

The time St. Jerome spent with Sacred Scripture led him to the conviction that "ignorance of Scripture is ignorance of Christ." St. Jerome spent twenty-one years translating the entire Bible into Latin. Originally, he translated it all from the Greek, and then went on to correct the Old Testament against the Hebrew original. There are so many words in the original Hebrew text of the Old Testament and Greek text of the New Testament that could have different meanings in Latin. Imagine the fervor with which he had to spend time in his heart with God in striving to make the proper translation.

For the next thousand years, his Latin Vulgate was the version of the Bible used by everyone in the Western world for their meditation. *Vulgate* means "in the common tongue." Latin was the common language throughout Western Europe at that time. Today the complete Bible has been translated into approximately seven hundred languages. The New Testament has been translated into well over 1,500 languages. It is indeed the greatest love letter of all time.

CONTEMPLATIVE PRAYER

Making our way back to the human relationship of Johnny and Susie, if things continue to progress, they will desire to communicate in a more intimate manner. This is where it gets exciting. In a kiss something of a person is made known that is not made known through words and thoughts.

It can be helpful to state the obvious about a kiss: it necessarily requires the free, mutual participation of two persons. Alone we might reflect on the memory of a past kiss. We could imagine what it would mean to kiss again. These thoughts about kissing are nothing in comparison to what happens in an actual kiss. In a kiss something is experienced that we cannot experience alone. There are different types of kisses: a kiss between lovers, a loving kiss given to a child or grandchild, even a kiss of peace given in church.

Each type of kiss communicates different things to the persons participating in it. Yet they all have this in common: For any kiss to communicate an authentic knowledge between the persons kissing, it cannot be forced. A kiss must be entered into mutually and freely.

Forcing a kiss on someone will not result in an intimate knowing of them. In fact, it may close their heart.

For a kiss to be a deep form of communication, it requires full, consensual attention. Talking will necessarily stop, and when the communication deepens, so will thoughts. A kiss can be the gateway to eventually "knowing someone" in the biblical sense. To "know" someone in the Bible refers to the intimacy of the marital embrace. In the marital embrace something even more profound will be communicated between the two persons now joined together by God. The *Catechism of the Catholic Church* helps us to appreciate how "conjugal love involves a totality, in which all the elements of the person enter.... [B]eyond union in one flesh, [it] leads to forming one heart and soul."[11]

Just as the kiss can eventually lead to the union of the marital embrace, contemplation is the gateway that will hopefully lead us to union with God, to "know fully, as I am fully known" (1 Cor. 13:12). Union with God is the ultimate end we hope for. To lead us to union with God, there is first what we might call the kiss of contemplation.

The Kiss of Contemplative Prayer

The Song of Songs begins with this first telling line: "Let him kiss me with kisses of his mouth" (1:2). Contemplation can be likened to a kiss between spouses, as something

---

[11] *Catechism of the Catholic Church*, no. 1643.

is experienced in contemplation that we cannot experience alone with our ideas. *Vocal prayer* might express what a great thing it is to know and be known by God. *Meditation* can try and deepen in our heart what we know of God, His thoughts, His ways, His will. Our imagination could do some pretty amazing things in meditation. It will all pale in comparison with the actual kiss of contemplation.

In contemplation, something of God is made known in a way that other forms of prayer can only lead to. As St. Teresa of Avila explains, "God so places Himself in the interior part of the soul that when it returns to itself, it can in no way doubt that it was in God and God was in it."[12]

There is something deeper of His own person that God is waiting and wanting to communicate to us. This is where prayer gets exciting.

Contemplative Prayer Is the Activity between Two Persons

Contemplative prayer or contemplation is something we cannot experience alone with our ideas. Contemplation comes from two Latin words: *con,* which means "with"; and *templum,* which is "a space cut out for God." Contemplation is that experience of prayer when we are aware that it is no longer the activity of just one person in our soul.

[12] St. Teresa of Avila, *The Interior Castle,* 5.1.9.

Contemplation is something I can only be disposed toward receiving, it is not something I can bring about on my own. Our Lord warned, "Not everyone who says to me, 'Lord, Lord,' will enter the kingdom of heaven" (Matt. 7:21). A wise monk observed that "you cannot be a mystic for the asking."[13]

St. John of the Cross goes so far as to say that "God does not bring to contemplation all those who purposely exercise themselves in the way of the spirit, nor even half. Why? God knows best."[14]

We cannot force God to kiss us with the kisses of His mouth. God reveals Himself in this intimate way, as St. Teresa of Avila observes, "when He desires, as He desires, and to whom He desires. Since these blessings belong to Him, He does no injustice to anyone."[15]

This should not come as a disappointment or discouragement. It authenticates even more how God is His own person. Within the intimate movements of this relationship, St. Teresa observes how the Lord gives such favors "in conformity with the love we have for Him."[16] To help manifest the authentic love we have for God, she gives the wise advice to do in prayer "that which best stirs

---

13   A Monk, *The Hermitage Within: Spirituality of the Desert*, trans. Alan Neame (London: Darton, Longman and Todd, 1999), p. 27.

14   St. John of the Cross, *The Dark Night*, in *The Collected Works of St. John of the Cross*, trans. Kieran Kavanaugh, O.C.D., and Otilio Rodriguez, O.C.D. (Washington, D.C.: ICS Publications, 1973), bk. 1, chap. 9, par. 9.

15   St. Teresa of Avila, *The Interior Castle*, 4.1.2.

16   Ibid., 3.1.7.

you to love."[17] What may happen from there will prove to be a very pivotal point in our life of prayer.

Let Your Mind Stop

When the slightest inclination then comes to put down what you are doing and close your eyes, do that. The kiss of contemplation may be coming. For the kiss to come, it is necessary for the talking to stop. When a deep kiss is coming, your thoughts too may cease. St. Teresa shares that, without His guiding hand, she "cannot understand how the mind can be stopped."[18]

Stopping our mind is what God does in prayer; it is what happens when He comes in for a deep kiss. "When His Majesty desires the intellect to stop," Teresa says, "He occupies it in another way and gives it a light so far above what we can attain that it remains absorbed."[19] In what she will call the "Prayer of Recollection," the hand of God draws our senses and faculties gently inward. Both St. Teresa of Avila and St. John of the Cross are careful to recognize the suspending of our senses as the work of God in a soul as it begins to receive His gift of contemplation.

St. Teresa describes in *The Interior Castle* how "the pain of distraction is felt when suspension does not accompany prayer."[20] St. John poetically pens in his poem

17   Ibid., 4.1.7.
18   Ibid., 4.3.4.
19   Ibid., 4.3.6.
20   Ibid., 4.1.11.

The Dark Night how "He wounded my neck, suspending all of my senses."[21] What exactly that wound might be is not known to us. Given the context, we know that it is a wound of love. We also know that when God wounds the neck with His love, the head will nod off, "suspending all of my senses." In the human experience of a deep kiss, some may experience getting weak in the knees. In this deep kiss of God, it would seem to be the neck. Remember, in this relationship with God, we do with Him as we would do with any other person. Then, since it is God, we do with Him what He alone can do.

Rest in His Love

By all outward appearances it will seem as if we have simply fallen asleep. We remain aware of what is going on around us. We will even question whether we are asleep, which I find is a good sign that I am not asleep. It eventually dawned on me that when I am sleeping, I never question whether I am asleep. I might wonder if I am dreaming, which is clarified when I awake. When the senses are being drawn gently inward and the head begins to nod off, it is important to be aware of what might be unfolding so that we may give our consent. Although contemplation is what God does in prayer, the kiss still takes two. Going back to the basics, a kiss requires the free, mutual participation of two people.

---

[21] St. John of the Cross, *The Dark Night,* Prologue for Reader, stanza 7.

Think of all the times God may be trying to come in for the kiss of contemplation, but we would not stop talking. Or when the deep kiss was coming, but we would not give our consent to looking like we were nodding off.

This may all come as new information to us. Unfortunately, not much has changed since St. Teresa reflected with her own sisters on how "we always hear about what a good thing prayer is, and our constitutions oblige us to spend many hours in prayer. Yet only what we ourselves can do in prayer is explained to us; little is explained about what the Lord does in a soul, I mean about the supernatural."[22]

How good to be reminded of "what the Lord does in a soul"—of how in prayer we are relating to the Person who created our souls, saves our souls, and desires to dwell in our souls. The possibilities of what God can do in prayer are truly infinite. The gateway to *union* with Him is being opened to us. Contemplation places us on the path to "know fully, as I am fully known" (1 Cor. 13:12).

The Church has long regarded St. John of the Cross as a soul who came to know God as the person He is. He was canonized a saint, named a Doctor of the Church, and given the specific title "Mystical Doctor," acknowledging the depth of his teaching on the soul's union with God. *And You Will Find Rest: What God Does in Prayer* is specifically aimed at appreciating what St. John of the

---

[22] St. Teresa of Avila, *The Interior Castle,* 1.2.7.

Cross relates about prayer in his work *The Dark Night*. The definition of contemplation he gives in *The Dark Night* is gone through in detail in *And You Will Find Rest*. It is a fitting way to conclude this reflection on *Knowing God* as we make our way soon to *Loving God*.

> *Contemplation is nothing*
> *else than a secret*
> *and peaceful and loving*
> *inflow of God, which,*
> *if not hampered, fires the*
> *soul in the spirit of love.*[23]

Contemplation Is "Secret"

It is a secret how the kiss of contemplation happens. We cannot make it happen on our own. The more we try to make it happen, the more it won't. When the deep kiss comes, it remains so much of a secret that St. Teresa of Avila comments on how the faculties are "looking in wonder at what they see."[24]

We may have experienced something of contemplation long before we studied how to pray. It is not unusual for a child to experience this "secret, peaceful, and loving inflow of God's love." Jesus did teach our need to become like children (Matt. 18:3). Children

---

[23] St. John of the Cross, *The Dark Night*, 1.10.6.
[24] St. Teresa of Avila, *The Interior Castle*, 4.2.6.

don't need to understand why they are receiving the gifts they are given. They readily accept them, even when they don't deserve them. Contemplation is a gift we could never earn. It requires humility to receive this gift that comes in such a mysterious way. There will be a childlike awe and wonder at what God now does in prayer. Contemplation is "secret."

Contemplation is "peaceful."

Contemplation is not unlike the experience of speaking a foreign language fluently. I lived in Italy for four years while studying for the priesthood and needed to learn some Italian. What I learned was an exhausting process of *translation*. I would hear what they said in Italian and try to translate it in my head into English. If I needed to make a reply, I would need to think of it in English and then translate it into Italian. There is another level at which a foreign language can be appreciated. When one is *fluent*, no translation is necessary. It comes *peacefully*.

Vocal prayer and meditation are not unlike the process of translation. In vocal prayer we take what we know in human terms and try to express it to the Divine. In meditation we attempt to take what has been divinely revealed and translate it into what we can humanly grasp. In contemplation, no translation is necessary. It comes *peacefully*. We are now *fluent* in the silent language of God.

To help distinguish between meditation and contemplation, St. Teresa of Avila uses the image of water filling a trough. In meditation "the water comes from far away through many aqueducts and the use of much ingenuity; with the other, the source of water is right there, and the trough fills without any noise."[25] Contemplation is "peaceful."

Contemplation is "loving."

As discussed earlier at length, contemplation is very much like the kiss one might enter into with one's spouse. In contemplation there is an experience of love that is beyond the capacity of what one person alone could experience. When this kiss of God is authentically experienced, St. John of the Cross will go so far as to claim, "a little of this pure love is more precious to God and the soul and more beneficial to the Church, even though it seems one is doing nothing, than all these other works put together."[26]

This is important to bear in mind, as it might seem like a big waste of time to sit and wait for a kiss. To "be still and know that I am God" (Ps. 46:11) is the risk made in the loving conviction that the "one who had made the promise was trustworthy" (Heb. 11:11). Contemplation is "loving."

---

[25] St. Teresa of Avila, *The Interior Castle*, 4.2.3.

[26] St. John of the Cross, *The Spiritual Canticle*, in *The Collected Works of St. John of the Cross*, stanza 29, par. 2.

Contemplation must not be "hampered."

There is a story of a man who was about to give an acceptance speech for an award being presented to him by his parish. While he was seated at the head table beside the parish priest, the man's wife passed him a note just prior to the presentation. Opening the note, he smiled as he saw the letters *K.I.S.S.*

Catching a glimpse of the note, the parish priest remarked to the man how precious it was that his wife would encourage him with a kiss before his speech. "It isn't what you think, Father," the man replied. "It stands for 'Keep It Simple, Stupid.'" This is also good advice for those longing to receive the "kisses of his mouth" (Song 1:2): Keep It Simple, Sinners.

When the kiss is about to come, when we sense "a gentle drawing inward"[27] by the Lord, we will need to resist the urge that will come to *hamper* this activity of God. I remember distinctly when this first began to unfold in prayer. I did not understand what was happening and would not give my consent. I was too prideful to look like I was sleeping while praying amidst other seminarians in our chapel. I did whatever I could to stay awake. I could have benefited from the wisdom of St. Teresa on how "doing something arduous would cause more harm than good.... Leave the soul in God's hands, let Him do whatever He wants with it."[28] How

---

27 St. Teresa of Avila, *The Interior Castle*, 4.3.3.
28 Ibid., 4.3.6.

important it is to be aware of how giving our consent to this "gentle drawing inward" by the Lord is much better than anything else we could do.

The author of *The Cloud of Unknowing* helps us to remember how "one loving blind desire for God alone is more valuable in itself, more pleasing to God and to the saints, more beneficial to your own growth, and more helpful to your friends, both living and dead, than anything else you could do."[29] Contemplation must be "not hampered."

Contemplation "fires the soul in a spirit of love."

In the Fifth Dwelling of her *Interior Castle*, St. Teresa uses the image of a silkworm to help us appreciate the fruit of what unfolds in this kiss of contemplation. A silkworm begins as an egg, and next develops as the weather warms into a worm, nourishing itself on twigs of mulberry trees. It then spins and encloses itself in a cocoon of silk. "The silkworm, which is fat and ugly, then dies; and a little white butterfly, which is very pretty, comes forth from the cocoon."[30]

For this kiss of contemplation to unfold, the soul will first begin to live by the warmth of the Holy Spirit through the remedies of the Church: going to Confession,

---

[29] *The Cloud of Unknowing* (Garden City, NY: Image Books, 1973), chap. 9, p. 60.
[30] St. Teresa of Avila, *The Interior Castle*, 5.2.2.

reading good books, and hearing homilies. They will come to know the Lord as the person He is.

As they learn to pray vocally and spend time in meditation, they will want to love the Lord for who He is and so strive to get "rid of self-love and self-will, our attachment to any earthly thing."[31] When they sense "a gentle drawing inward"[32] by the Lord, they will give their consent. And when at last "the soul is, in this prayer, truly dead to the world, a little white butterfly comes forth. Oh, the greatness of God! How transformed the soul is when it comes out of this prayer after having been placed within the greatness of God and so closely joined with Him for a little while."[33]

Let us never underestimate "what God has prepared for those who love Him" (1 Cor. 2:9). I remember meeting with a person for spiritual direction. When our time concluded a little early, they went on to visit about other matters. I stopped them with an invitation to go into the church before the Blessed Sacrament with the time that was remaining. They responded that by the time they arrived, there would only be about ten minutes. I encouraged them not to underestimate what God can do in ten minutes. To this day they remain a messenger to others of "the greatness of God" and what He can do in ten minutes.

---

[31] Ibid., 5.2.6.
[32] Ibid., 4.3.3.
[33] Ibid., 5.2.7.

So often I go into prayer as the fat, ugly silkworm, burdened by budgets, exhausted by health, worried about relationships. Then, as only God can do in prayer, He draws me into His rest and allows me to emerge refreshed, renewed in a way that a few minutes of sleep could never do.

Having been drawn into the kiss of contemplative prayer, the soul will emerge with the two beautiful virtues of *humility* and *charity*. Humility is born from an awareness that a gift of God's love has been received that is way beyond our ability to earn. This, in turn, "fires the soul in the spirit of love." Since we have received what we could not earn, we are now on fire to be more charitable to our neighbor. St. Teresa assures us that we can "be certain that the more advanced you see you are in love for your neighbor, the more advanced you will be in the love of God."[34] A very fitting line to now transition to our next reflection, on *Loving God*.

[34] Ibid., 5.3.8.

LOVING GOD

To write on *Loving God* was much more of a task than I imagined it might be. I was consoled to learn that one of the more engaging works on love, by Josef Pieper, was his most difficult work. There is a volume today that combines his three separate works on Faith, Hope, and Love. In it, he articulates how he struggled for years with the one on love and almost abandoned the effort. He published the first of the three, *On Hope*, in 1935. *On Love* was finally completed in 1972, thirty-seven years later.[35]

My own process of preparing to write on *Loving God* drew me back to a story I once heard about Mahatma Gandhi. A mother in India was upset that her son was eating too much sugar. No matter how much she chided him, he continued to satisfy his sweet tooth. Totally frustrated, she decided to take him to the person she knew he respected. It was a long journey on foot.

When they arrived, she respectfully approached Mahatma Gandhi. "Sir, my son eats too much sugar. It is not good for his health. Would you please advise him

---

[35] Josef Pieper, *Faith–Hope–Love* (San Francisco: Ignatius Press, 1997), p. 9.

to stop eating it?" Gandhi listened carefully to the woman, then turned to her son and said, "Go home and come back in two weeks."

The woman was perplexed. Why hadn't Gandhi spoken to her son that day about eating too much sugar? Respectfully, she returned two weeks later with her son. Upon their arrival, Gandhi motioned for them to come forward. He looked intently at the boy and said, "Boy, you should stop eating sugar. It is not good for your health." The boy was struck by the sincerity of Gandhi and promised he would not continue this habit any longer. The boy's mother turned to Gandhi and asked, "Why didn't you tell him that two weeks ago when I brought him here to see you?" Gandhi smiled, "Two weeks ago I was still eating sugar myself. Before I could tell your son to stop eating sugar, I had to stop eating sugar first."

In a similar fashion, before writing to others about *Loving God*, I realized the need to first take a good, long look at my own love for God. In taking that look, the Lord was eager to shed His light upon certain shadows that can cloud an authentic love for who He truly is.

Perhaps, like many of us, I first learned to love God as the Giver of gifts. I loved Him for the food that I was about to receive, for the gift of my life, for my family, for all creation. I loved Him for His blessings and His grace. I loved God as the Giver of every good gift. In the Third Eucharistic Prayer of Holy Mass we rightly pray of "Christ Our Lord, through whom you bestow on the world all that is good."

Loving God as the Giver of gifts is a good first start, although it can tend to be sentimental. When we receive the gifts we enjoy, our feeling of love for God can be strong. On the other hand, when we do not receive the gifts for which we ask exactly as we anticipate, our feelings of love can wane.

"Love," Benedict XVI reflected in his encyclical letter on this subject, "is not merely a sentiment. Sentiments come and go. A sentiment can be a marvelous first spark, but it is not the fullness of love."[36]

In the story of the rich young man, his initial sentiments of love were a marvelous first spark that stirred him to run up to Jesus, kneel down, and enthusiastically ask, "Good teacher, what must I do to inherit eternal life?" (Mark 10:17). How beautiful it would have been for that spark to fan into a flame of recognizing the Gift standing right there before him. To see Jesus as the one thing he was lacking, for whom he would readily sell everything to enter into a relationship. It is one thing to love God as the Giver of gifts. It is quite another to recognize Him as the Gift, the treasure that "out of joy" one "goes and sells all that he has" to obtain (Matt. 13:44). Unfortunately, his love for Jesus was not yet the fullness of love; it was a sentiment that came and went.

---

[36] Benedict XVI, encyclical letter *Deus Caritas Est: God Is Love* (December 25, 2005), no. 17.

As Jesus walked by John the Baptist, John observed to two of his disciples, "Behold, the Lamb of God" (John 1:36). Mr. Wonderful had entered the room. That stirred a marvelous first spark in Philip[37] and Andrew, compelling them to run up to Jesus. When Jesus saw them following Him, He turned and asked, "What are you looking for?" (John 1:38).

Looking for Love

It is the question Jesus asks every prospective disciple. What is igniting this marvelous first spark? Is this a sentimental search for a Giver of gifts? Or have you recognized in your heart the one thing you are lacking, the treasure that "out of joy" one "goes and sells all that he has" to obtain?

[37] *The Navarre Bible: The Gospel of John* (Dublin: Four Courts Press, 1997), p. 56, footnote for John 1:40–41, explains how "we cannot be absolutely sure who the second disciple was." The *Navarre* commentary goes on to explain that "since the very earliest centuries of the Christian era, he has always been taken to be the evangelist himself. The vividness of the account, the detail of giving the exact time, and even John's tendency to remain anonymous (cf. 19:16, 20:2, 21:7, 20) seem to confirm this." It could also be argued that the second disciple is Philip, for the Gospel of John continues in verse 43 to have Jesus going the next day to find Philip in Galilee. In verse 45 it is Philip who tells Nathanael, "We have found the one about whom Moses wrote in the law, and also the prophets, Jesus, son of Joseph, from Nazareth." In verse 46, Philip invites Nathanael with the same words that Jesus had addressed to the two disciples of John in verse 39, "Come and see." While I share the view of *The Navarre Bible: The Gospel of John* that "we cannot be absolutely sure who the second disciple was," I have chosen to identify the second disciple as Philip.

When Jesus asked them this question, Philip and Andrew gave the right response: "Rabbi, ... where are you staying?" (John 1:38). They simply wanted to be with Jesus. Jesus then pursues them and says, "Come, and you will see." Accepting His invitation, "they went and saw where he was staying, and they stayed with him that day" (John 1:39).

What are we looking for? Most of us are looking for love. We have many ideas about love, ideas about how we would like to love and be loved. And yet not everyone's ideas on love are a match. Dr. Gary Chapman identified five different "love languages." He has helped countless couples realize that we express and receive love in ways we find most meaningful to us, through Physical Touch, Words of Affirmation, Acts of Service, Quality Time, and Gift Giving.[38]

In the English language, the word *love* is used with many different meanings. We love chocolate, we love our parents, we love puppy dogs, we love the weather, we love how someone looks, we love how they make us feel, we love by a conscious act of the will to do what is good for another by sacrificing for them. When someone says, "I love you," what do they really mean? The Greek language in which the New Testament was written can be helpful here, as it has different words for love. Three of them are relevant to share.

---

[38] Gary Chapman, *The 5 Love Languages: The Secret to Love That Lasts* (Chicago: Northfield Publishing, 2015).

Eros is a love that affirms the goodness of a person through our desire to want to be with them. C. S. Lewis helps us appreciate how "Eros makes a man really want, not a woman, but one particular woman.... [T]he lover desires the Beloved herself, not the pleasure she can give."[39] Eros is a passionate love that seeks with sensual desire and longing. It is used only twice in Sacred Scripture, both times in the Old Testament.

Philia is a love that affirms the goodness of a person based more on their virtues. It is a more practical love that sees things the same way as another. It is the word used for friendship. The ancient quote of the Roman statesman Sallust on friendship is helpful here: "To desire the same things and to reject the same things constitutes true friendship." While eros will make you feel your nerves "tugging at your guts and fluttering in your diaphragm," C. S. Lewis memorably writes, "in Friendship — in that luminous, tranquil, rational world of relationships freely chosen — you got away from all that. This alone, of all the loves, seemed to raise you to the level of gods or angels."[40] Philia is the word found in the Gospel of John to express the relationship between Jesus and His disciples.

Agape is a pure, unconditional love. Agape is a love that affirms the goodness of a person through what we

---

[39] C. S. (Clive Staples) Lewis, *The Four Loves* (New York: Harper-Collins, 1960), p. 121.

[40] Ibid., p. 75.

are freely willing to sacrifice for their good. Agape is the good news of the love of Jesus Christ. Agape is the primary word for love in the New Testament, found over a hundred times as a verb and nearly as many times as a noun.

There can be a temptation to set eros and agape in opposition to each other, which is unfortunate. Eros is a love somehow rooted in our human nature, as in the first Adam who seeks Eve as the one who "at last, is bone of my bones and flesh of my flesh" (Gen. 2:23). Agape then guards our passions toward seeking the true good for this one we have sought out, as in the Second Adam (1 Cor. 15:45), Jesus, whose "Passion" led Him to seek us out to save us. Eros has sparked many men, like the first Adam, to "leave his father and mother and cling to his wife" (Gen. 2:24). Agape is then able to guard that spark as it is fanned into the flame of the love we see in the last Adam, Jesus, who "loved the church and handed himself over for her to sanctify her" (Eph. 5:25–26).

Benedict XVI helps us to appreciate how "God loves, and His love may certainly be called *eros,* yet it is also totally *agape.*"[41] In Jesus, we see the perfect blend of eros and agape as Jesus seeks out His bride to save her by laying down His life for her. It is the fullness of love that will pull us out of ourselves, from merely clinging to another for the gifts we might like to receive from them, to loving "as Christ loved the church and handed himself

---

[41] Benedict XVI, *Deus Caritas Est*, no. 9.

over for her to sanctify her." The *other* we encounter is so wonderful that we lose ourselves. We recognize them as the gift, the one thing we are lacking, the person for whom we are willing to give up everything.

This is the love God has for us. The Second Person of the Blessed Trinity empties Himself (Phil. 2:7) to be with us. Have you ever stopped to consider what love it must have taken for God to become a man? To give up everything He had experienced as God to become a man and live on earth? *The Word*—through whom all things came into being—so emptied Himself that He had to be taught how to speak. The One who held all of creation in His hands needed to cry to be picked up and held in the arms of one He had created.

There is a story told by the well-known radio host Paul Harvey about a man who just couldn't bring himself to believe that God became man and lived on earth.[42] As his wife was preparing to leave for the midnight celebration of Christmas Eve, he stayed home, explaining that he would feel hypocritical accompanying her. As he settled into his fireside chair, a snowstorm began to blow in. Not long afterward, he heard a steadily increasing thudding sound outside, almost like the sound of snowballs being thrown at his home.

When he went to the front door to investigate, he found a flock of birds huddled miserably in the snow.

---

[42] Paul Harvey, "The Man and the Birds," ABC Radio, December 24, 2004. The story is adapted here for the sake of brevity.

They had been caught in the storm and, in a desperate search for shelter, had been trying to fly through his large landscape window. The sight of these poor creatures in danger of freezing moved his heart. He trudged through the deepening snow to help guide them into the warmth of his barn. He opened wide the doors to the barn and turned on the light, but the birds did not come in.

The man went back to the house to get some breadcrumbs to entice them, sprinkling a trail on the ground to lead them to the barn. But the birds just ignored them and continued to flap helplessly in the snow. He tried shooing them into the barn, walking around them and waving his arms as they scattered in every direction, except into the warm, lighted barn. He realized they were afraid of him. *If only I could think of some way to let them know they can trust me, that I am not trying to hurt them.* But how? They just would not follow.

Then it dawned upon him. *If only I could be a bird and mingle with them and speak their language, then I could tell them not to be afraid. Then I could show them the way to the safe, warm barn. But I would have to be one of them, so they could see and hear and understand.* At that moment the church bells began to ring with the glad tidings of Christmas, "O come let us adore Him," and he sank to his knees in the snow.

It would be hard to imagine a man who so loved birds that he would leave everything he experiences as a man to become a bird and live with them. Then let us realize that, as much as our human experience is above that of a bird, God is infinitely higher than a human. Hopefully this helps us to begin to appreciate the type of eros that moved God to become a man and the agape that compelled Him to lay down His life so that we might enter into union with Him.

When Two Become One

There are two relationships in which we speak of union, of the two becoming one: the union between a man and woman in the sacrament of Holy Matrimony and our union with God. Marital union is an *image* to help us appreciate the *reality* of our union with God. It is an image in the sense that the physical relationship between a man and woman is passing, but our union with God will never pass away.

The prophecies of Hosea (2:16–22), Ezekiel (16:6–14), and Isaiah (54:4–6) use the metaphor of marriage to describe the relationship between God and His people. The book of Revelation describes the Second Coming of Christ as the "wedding day of the Lamb" (Rev. 19:7). Jesus compares the Kingdom of Heaven to a wedding feast (Matt. 22:1–14) and warns us of our need to be ready to greet the Bridegroom (Matt. 25:1–13). St. Paul sets Christ before us as our one true husband (2 Cor. 11:2) and likens the relationship between Christ and the Church to that of a marriage (Eph. 5:23).

I have found it helpful to think of marriage as like a *photograph* of the Bahamas and union with God as like *being* in the Bahamas. A photograph is nice to have, to hang on your wall and let it inspire you to get to the Bahamas. When you arrive there, it will not even dawn on you to look at the picture, because you are immersed in the beauty of being in the Bahamas. In Heaven, no one is going to miss the marital embrace. It will not even dawn on us to tell God how it might be a lot better in Heaven if we just had sex twice a week. Union with God is infinitely beyond the experience of human intimacy. As St. Paul was able to help us appreciate, "When the perfect comes, the partial will pass away.... At present I know partially; then I shall know fully, as I am fully known" (1 Cor. 13:10, 12).

To help impress this truth upon us, God calls some to renounce human sexuality. Why? It is not because human sexuality is bad. God created human sexuality as a beautiful, good gift—yet there is something greater. It is "for the sake of the kingdom of heaven" (Matt. 19:12) that some renounce the pleasure of the marital embrace. But for most humans, the marital embrace will help guide them along the way to the union we hope to enjoy in our heavenly homeland (Heb. 11:16).

Now, the evil one does everything in his power to try and tarnish this good gift of sexuality. He wants to destroy the very image we are given to guide us toward eternal intimacy with God. And he has done (and continues to do) a very convincing job of getting us to regard sex as something much different than God created it to be. Some might think that sex is naughty or dirty; others would find it strange to bring God into the marital embrace. How did that happen? That certainly did not come from God. How God must grieve over the many relationships, the marriages, that experience deep turmoil over this beautiful gift. How deeply God must long for us to appreciate this gift for what it was created to be.

I often joke that perhaps God created sex as too pleasurable. If He had kept that experience at the level of a nice, warm bath, perhaps we would have all been a lot safer. But God is so good! It is no secret to Him how pleasurable it is. He made it that way. Imagine the joy it brought God to bestow on us this act that would help us appreciate our union with Him and root us in the truth of how the creation of new life is an act of love, His love. He knew we would really, really like this gift. Would it not be fitting to at least give thanks to God together after the marital embrace, something as simple as saying, "How great Thou art"?

There is a danger, perhaps more prevalent than ever, that our ability to experience real love will be hampered, if not blocked permanently. That was the observation of Josef Pieper, who articulated the danger of when "sexual activity [is] separated from eros."[43]

---

[43] Pieper, *Faith–Hope–Love*, p. 264.

The deadly sin of lust can so twist a person that they are unable to truly love.

The Distortion of Lust

Sexual activity can mistakenly be regarded as the height of the human experience of love. It is not. C. S. Lewis helps us to appreciate how "Sexual desire, without Eros, wants *it*, the *thing in itself*; Eros wants the Beloved. The *thing* is a sensory pleasure; that is, an event within one's own body."[44] "The mere sex partner," Pieper observed, "does not come into focus as a personal being."[45] Lewis portrays this in the "lustful man prowling the streets, [who says] that he 'wants a woman.' Strictly speaking, a woman is just what he does not want. He wants a pleasure for which a woman happens to be the necessary piece of apparatus. How much he cares about the woman as such may be gauged by his attitude to her five minutes after fruition."[46]

When sexual activity is separated from eros, our ability to love authentically is damaged, maybe forever. Pieper soberingly observes how when "sex enters youths' consciousness and life before eros does ... experiencing real love is hampered if not blocked permanently."[47] In separating sexual activity from eros, "the fig leaf has merely been moved to another place; it now covers the

---

[44]   Lewis, *The Four Loves*, pp. 120–121.
[45]   Pieper, *Faith–Hope–Love*, p. 265.
[46]   Lewis, *The Four Loves*, p. 121.
[47]   Pieper, *Faith–Hope–Love*, p. 264.

human face."[48] The fig leaf was originally carefully placed to protect the dignity of the person. Their face remained in clear view. The fig leaf is now often intentionally moved, particularly in advertising and in the media, to disregard the person, to cover their face and see only a mere object of our personal pleasure.

The evil one knew that in moving the fig leaf to cover the face of the human person, the challenge of seeking the face of God would become all the greater. That is worth repeating.

> *By moving the fig leaf to cover the face of a human person, the evil one knew that it would become even more difficult for us to seek the face of God.*

Is Eros an Embrace — or an Escape?

An eros that is not anchored in agape can carry us away from experiencing authentic love. Great care must be taken to ensure that it is the marital embrace being sought and not a mere sexual escape. To embrace means to take into one's arms. To escape is to flee suffering by stepping "out of one's cape." The embrace is an *in;* the escape is an *out.* How fulfilling the experience of taking into one's arms the commitment of being faithful in good times and bad, sickness and health, till death do they part, rather than

---

[48] Ibid., p. 265.

merely looking for a moment's escape from the hardships of life by stepping out of one's capes.

When approached the right way, the marital embrace will anchor you more deeply together in the love of God. This is the whole purpose of marriage, a purpose that will not pass away. What a different world it would be if the aim of every husband was to love his wife "as Christ loved the church and handed himself over for her to sanctify her" (Eph. 5:25–26). That is the world God created it to be, a world He will never give up on. It is the world that will be when the true Bridegroom returns for His bride.

There is much that we could explore concerning human sexuality. If you would like to read further on this topic, I would refer you to Josef Pieper's work *On Love* and C. S. Lewis's *The Four Loves*.

Seeing Love Clearly

Returning to the question of Jesus, "What are you looking for?" (John 1:38), we hope to preserve the desire expressed in Psalm 27, "Your face, LORD, do I seek" (v. 8). We seek the face of persons, not ideas. The Beatitude, the blessing we are given in seeking the face of God, is purity of heart: "Blessed are the pure in heart, they shall see God" (Matt. 5:8 NJB).

There is nothing more tragic than allowing the impurity of our heart to put a fig leaf over the face of God. When we seek God to merely satisfy our own pleasure, our ability to experience real love is hampered, if not blocked permanently. We see this in the story of the rich young man. He was hampered, if not blocked permanently, from seeing the face of God. Among the pleasures he had come to enjoy in his many possessions, he was seeking to add the pleasure of being assured by Jesus that he had done what was necessary to inherit eternal life. With the face of Jesus standing right there before him, the fig leaf of seeking this pleasure from Jesus blocked his view as he walked away sad from the relationship that is eternal life.

Building a Foundation of Love

In advising her sisters on prayer, St. Teresa of Avila gives the wise counsel that "souls shouldn't be thinking about consolations at this beginning stage. It would be a very poor way to start building so precious and great an edifice. If the foundation is on sand, the whole building will fall to the ground. They'll never finish being dissatisfied and tempted."[49] She continues her instruction: "The whole aim of any person who is beginning prayer — and don't forget this because it's very important — should be that he work and prepare himself with determination and every possible effort to bring his will into conformity with God's will."[50]

[49] St. Teresa of Avila, *The Interior Castle*, 2.1.7.
[50] Ibid., 2.1.8.

The rich young man had asked what must be done. When told by God what he should do, he made no effort to bring his will into conformity with God's will. The foundation on which he had built up his hope for eternal life was on the sand of seeking consolation and pleasure, and the whole building fell to the ground.

If we want to place our feet on a sound foundation, then we should take great care to heed these important three steps that Jesus carefully marked off for anyone who is experiencing that marvelous first spark to follow Him. "If anyone wishes to come after me," Jesus said, "he must

1) deny himself

2) and take up his cross daily

3) and follow me" (Luke 9:23).

Jesus knows that our being drawn to Him can be a good, initial, sentimental spark. He also knows, as did St. Teresa of Avila, that "we love ourselves very much."[51] For that spark to be fanned into a flame of authentic love, it will need to be disciplined and purified.

St. Teresa is careful to teach how for the deeper movements of prayer to unfold, "the initial thing necessary for such favors is to love God without self-interest."[52] This echoes the great anthem of love by St. Paul, who while

[51] Ibid., 5.4.6.
[52] Ibid., 4.2.9.

proclaiming how love is "patient," "kind," and not "jealous," "pompous," "inflated," or "rude," is also clear on how love "does not seek its own interests" (1 Cor. 13:4–5).

St. Bernard of Clairvaux complements this by helping us to appreciate how

> love is a great reality, but there are degrees to it. The bride stands at the highest. Children love their father, but they are thinking of their inheritance; and as long as they have any fear of losing it, they honor more than they love the one from whom they expect to inherit. I suspect the love which seems to be founded on some hope of gain. It is weak, for if the hope is removed, it may be extinguished or at least diminished. It is not pure, as it desires some return. Pure love has no self-interest. Pure love does not gain strength through expectation, nor is it weakened by distrust. This is the love of the bride, for this is the bride—with all that means.[53]

The love of the bride, with all that means, was seen beautifully in Mother Teresa. In her private writings, she painfully expressed how her love for God was being

[53] St. Bernard of Clairvaux, *On the Song of Songs*, vol. 4, trans. Irene Edmonds (Kalamazoo, MI: Cistercian Publications, 1980), Sermon 83, pp. 184–185.

purified. Amid her dryness in prayer, with God seeming so absent, her love became so pure, so free of self-interest, that she writes how she was willing to accept this suffering "to the end of life."[54] In fact, she goes so far as to say, "I am willing with all my heart to suffer all that I suffer — not only now — but for all eternity — if this is possible. Your happiness is all that I want."[55] In this heartfelt statement, we get a glimpse of what "one loving blind desire for God alone" can look like. This was described earlier for us by the author of *The Cloud of Unknowing,* who went on to stress the importance of what we cannot hear enough, how this "one loving blind desire for God alone is more valuable in itself, more pleasing to God and to the saints, more beneficial to your own growth, and more helpful to your friends, both living and dead, than anything else you could do."[56] It is "a little of this pure love," which we heard earlier from St. John of the Cross, who similarly stressed, "is more precious to God and the soul and more beneficial to the Church, even though it seems one is doing nothing, than all the other works put together."[57]

This is what it can look like when Jesus is very clearly the one thing we are lacking, the person for whom we are willing to give up everything. "This is the

---

[54] St. Teresa of Calcutta, *Come Be My Light.* (New York: Doubleday, 2007), p. 188.

[55] Ibid., p. 194.

[56] *Cloud of Unknowing,* chap. 9, p. 60.

[57] St. John of the Cross, *The Spiritual Canticle,* stanza 29, par. 2.

love of the bride, for this is the bride—with all that means," St. Bernard beautifully continues, for "love is the being and the hope of a bride. She is full of it, and the bridegroom is contented with it. He asks nothing else, and she has nothing else to give. That is why he is the bridegroom and she the bride; this love is the property only of the couple. No one else can share it, not even a son."[58]

This is the Bride of Christ we hope to become more fully.

We are children of Our Father in Heaven. That truth is marked on our very soul through Baptism. Let us also never miss how we are the chosen Bride of Christ. That truth is made beautifully manifest in every celebration of Holy Mass.

The Sacrament of Love[59]

In the sacrament of the Most Holy Eucharist, God seeks us out as His own dear bride, to lay down His life out of love for us. This is the reality that happens right before our very eyes at every single Mass. At the beginning of Mass, the priest invites us to "prepare ourselves to celebrate these sacred mysteries." What happens at Mass is a

---

[58] St. Bernard of Clairvaux, *On the Song of Songs*, vol. 4, Sermon 83, p. 185.

[59] Benedict XVI, post-synodal apostolic exhortation *Sacramentum Caritatis*: The Sacrament of Charity (February 22, 2007), no. 1. Benedict cites St. Thomas Aquinas, *Summa Theologica* III, q. 73, a. 3.

"mystery." It transcends time and space. It is also "sacred," for at every Mass the Bridegroom lays down His life for His bride. The Passion, Death, and Resurrection of Jesus Christ is made present at every Mass.

What happens at Mass is not a sentimental, dramatic reenactment of what once happened in the life of Christ. The Council of Trent clarifies how, "in this divine sacrifice, which is celebrated in the Mass, the same Christ who offered himself once in a bloody manner on the altar of the cross is contained and is offered in an unbloody manner." "The victim is one and the same: the same now offers through the ministry of priests, who then offered himself on the cross; only the manner of offering is different."[60]

It is Christ speaking through the priest who stands *in persona Christi,* saying what only Christ can efficaciously say: "This is my Body, which will be given up for you." In our first reflection on *Knowing God,* I mentioned that in this relationship with the Father and the Son and the Holy Spirit, we do with God what we might do in any other intimate relationship. Then, since it is God, we do with Him what is unique to this relationship.

This is true in a very special way at the Holy Mass. What happens there between the Bride of Christ and the Bridegroom is beyond our wildest comprehension. It is beyond what eye can see, ear can hear, what could enter

---

[60] Council of Trent, "Doctrine on the Most Holy Sacrifice," as quoted in *Catechism of the Catholic Church,* no. 1367.

the human mind. Yet for those who love Him, love Him as His bride, it is a glimpse and a taste of "what God has prepared for those who love him" (1 Cor. 2:9). Receiving Holy Communion is what we refer to as the *consummation* of Mass: two become one. The same word is used in the sacrament of Holy Matrimony. In the consummation of a marriage, God does what only He can do in drawing a man and woman so intimately into His love that the two become one.

In Holy Communion, the prayer of Jesus — "That the love with which you loved me may be in them and I in them" (John 17:26), "I in them and you in me" (John 17:23) — is consummated. Into our body, blood, soul, and humanity we receive the Body, Blood, Soul, and Divinity of Our Lord Jesus Christ. The two become one. "Oh, the greatness of God!" St. Teresa exclaimed.[61] As St. Augustine came to recognize, "If we receive the Eucharist worthily, we become what we receive."[62]

Becoming What We Receive

At one level it is helpful to appreciate that God made every fiber of our being. He knows what we eat goes into our stomach, what goes into our stomach will enter our blood, and our blood then goes to our heart and is pumped to every part of our body. Each drop of blood passes through our heart every forty-five seconds. Our

---

[61] St. Teresa of Avila, *The Interior Castle*, 5.2.7.
[62] Easter Sermon, 227.

heart will send that blood to our brain, our eyes, our ears, our hands, and our feet.

A doctor can take a little bit of our blood and tell us if we have been eating the right foods. Are we eating bananas and apricots that give potassium, which is good for our hearing? Are we eating carrots and spinach that give vitamin A, which is good for our eyes? Are we eating fish, chicken, and eggs with vitamin B, which is good for our brain?

God knows all this. He made us this way. So He invites us to "Take and eat; this is my body" and "Drink from it, all of you, for this is my blood" (Matt. 26:26, 27).

The Eucharist is the superfood par excellence. The detox beyond our wildest expectations. To help prepare himself for these sacred mysteries, St. Thomas Aquinas would pray, "Loving Father, as on my earthly pilgrimage I now receive Your beloved Son under the veil of a sacrament, may I one day see him face to face in glory, who lives and reigns with You for ever."

What Am I Looking For ... at Mass?

Over the face of a bride is placed, not a fig leaf, but a veil. A veil to uphold with deep respect the dignity of the person we seek, with great anticipation of the veil being lifted, so that the long-desired union may one day be fully entered face-to-face. As St. Paul reminds us, "At present we see indistinctly, as in a mirror, but then face to face" (1 Cor. 13:12).

Under the veil of a sacrament, we are invited, as were Philip and Andrew by John the Baptist, to "Behold, the Lamb of God" (John 1:36). Then, like Philip and Andrew, let us allow the Bridegroom to turn to us and ask, "What are you looking for?" (John 1:38)

What are we looking for … in Mass? Are we looking for our heavenly inheritance, as a son or daughter of Our Father in Heaven? Are we looking for our Bridegroom, who has laid down His life for us?

As I look back, I can honestly recognize how I first prepared myself to celebrate these "sacred mysteries" very much as a son. In striking similarity to the rich young man, I was "thinking of my inheritance." To gain heaven, to inherit eternal life, I knew I needed to go to Mass. It was that type of love that is founded on some hope of gain, warned of by St. Bernard.

When we come to Mass looking to "get something out of it," our love for Mass will remain at a very senti-mental level. We will tend to measure our experience of Mass by how we feel. How did the music make me feel? How did the homily make me feel? How reverently did I feel it was being celebrated? When we don't get the feel-ing we were hoping for, it might seem as if we "didn't get anything out of Mass," or that "Mass was boring," as otherwise, we go through the same routine each time.

In striking similarity, the intimate activity between an earthly bride and bridegroom is pretty much the same thing every time, too. How unimaginably insulting it would be for your spouse to say to you, "I did not get much out of it," after you had just offered yourself entirely to your beloved!

Let us then realize that to say "we do not get anything out of Mass" is perhaps the deepest insult we could give to Jesus Christ. It would be placing the fig leaf squarely over His face. For in Mass, at every Mass, Jesus gives us Himself.

Let us never lose sight of what God is doing in the celebration of Holy Mass. Regardless of how we might feel about the music, the homily, the priest, the parish, we must strive to keep our eyes open to see how the Bridegroom just laid down His life to sanctify us. Let us not allow the fig leaf to block us from seeing what is really happening before our very eyes by tempting us to seek some type of personal pleasure at Mass.

I recently celebrated my eleven thousandth Mass. If anyone might be bored with Mass, it could be me. What same thing do we do eleven thousand times and not get bored with? Far from being bored, this is what gets me out of bed in the morning. Even when I'm sick, even the day of and after major surgeries. By God's grace, in the past twenty-seven years of being a priest, there are only twenty-seven days on which I have not celebrated Holy Mass: the twenty-seven Good Fridays on which we do not celebrate Mass as we are in the midst of the Sacred Triduum. What drives a man to do this? It is the grace to see, under the veil of this sacrament, Jesus, and to recognize in my heart that He is the one thing I am lacking.

Under the veil of a sacrament, let us strive to appreciate, along with St. Paul, how "Christ loved the church and handed himself over for her to sanctify her, cleansing her by the bath of water with the word, that he might present to himself the church in splendor, without spot or wrinkle or any such thing, that she might be holy and without blemish" (Eph. 5:25–27).

To be made without spot or wrinkle or any such thing is what will happen when we are truly *Loving God.* God, as a person, is love. God, as a person, is our Savior. To love Him as the person He is, we must allow Him to go where we need His love and where we are in need of being saved.

Loving God with a Pure Heart

In a letter written toward the end of his life, St. John of the Cross was helping a soul to realize that "where there is no love, put love, and you will draw out love."[63] This is what we are able to appreciate as happening in our relationship with God. "God is love" (1 John 4:8). Where there is no love in us, God will come to put His love, so that from that very place, He can draw out love. For this to happen, we must allow God to go where there is no

---

[63] St. John of the Cross, Letter 26 to Madre Maria de la Encarnacion in Segovia, July 6, 1591, in *The Collected Works of St. John of the Cross.*

love in us; to give our consent for God to love out of us all that is not of Him. The purity of heart with which we hope to see God is, in the end, God's work in us. "A clean heart create for me, God" (Ps. 51:12). It is He, we hear prophesied in the book of Ezekiel, who will "give them a new heart," removing from their bodies "the stony heart" (11:19). The path by which our heart is made pure by God is referred to as the passive purifications. Passive, for it is the work of God purifying our heart, a work we are free to either give our consent to or walk away from.

In a letter to a group of Carthusians, William of St. Thierry acknowledged that giving our consent "is no slight matter, no easy goal."[64] A monk once remarked on how "the passive purifications of the mystics is no joke, any more than the purgatory through which most of us will have to go."[65] For most of us, it will be in Purgatory that God creates in us a pure heart. Benedict XVI wrote,

> I would go so far to say that if there was no purgatory, then we would have to invent it, for who would dare say of himself that he was able to stand directly before God. And yet we don't want to be, to use an image from Scripture, "a pot that turned out wrong," that has to be thrown away; we want to be able to be put right. Purgatory

[64] William of St. Thierry, *The Golden Epistle*, p. 14.
[65] A Monk, *The Hermitage Within*, p. 56.

basically means that God can put the pieces back together again, that He can cleanse us in such a way that we are able to be with Him and can stand there in the fullness of life.... It strips off from one person what is unbearable and from another the inability to bear certain things, so that in each of them *a pure heart* is revealed, and we can see that we all belong together in one enormous symphony of being.[66]

It is the work of God's love that "can put the pieces back together again," that "strips off from one person what is unbearable and from another the inability to bear certain things. So that in each of them *a pure heart* is revealed." *Loving God* consists in giving our consent to allowing His love to purify our heart in this way now. To "cleanse us in such a way that we are able to be with Him" now! This can only be done by the hand of God. Yet, because it is the work of love, it takes two. We remain free to either give or withhold our consent to this work of God in our soul. Giving our consent to these passive purifications is, again, "no joke," "no slight matter, no easy goal."[67] William of St. Thierry then goes on with great care to assure us that

<hr>

[66] Benedict XVI, *God and the World: A Conversation with Peter Seewald* (San Francisco: Ignatius Press, 2002), pp. 130–131.

[67] William of St. Thierry, *The Golden Epistle*, p. 14.

> He who, in His love, makes you such prom-
> ises is almighty and good. He will be faithful
> in fulfilling them and untiring in giving
> help. To those who in their great love for
> Him pledge themselves to great things and,
> believing and trusting in His grace, under-
> take what is beyond their own strength, He
> imparts both the will and desire; and He
> follows up the grace to will by bestowing
> also the power to achieve.[68]

It is beyond our strength to have a pure heart. It is the work of God to even inspire in us a desire for Him to purify our heart now. *Loving God* then ultimately consists in allowing Him to love out of me all that is not of Him. Why? Because that is who He is; God is love, God is Savior. A wise monk observes that "God needs nothing of our wealth. But He does need our poverty, through which, alone, we may receive His gifts, His love, Himself. God is not able to be Himself, to be love, if He is not able to be self-outpouring into our hearts in the extrava-gant folly of His gratuitous love."[69]

How beautiful is that! All God wants to do is love us. All God needs from us to receive His love is our poverty. He waits for us to come to Him with empty hands so that we might "receive His gifts, His love,

---

[68] Ibid., pp. 14–15.

[69] A Carthusian, *The Way of Silent Love* (London: Darton, Longman and Todd, 1994), p. 28.

Himself." It is indeed the "extravagant folly of His gratuitous love."

St. John of the Cross sadly observes how "it is a matter of deep sorrow that while God had bestowed upon them the power to break with other stronger cords of attachments, they fail to attain so much good because they do not become detached from some childish thing which God has requested them to conquer out of love for Him." How "regrettable, then, to behold some souls, laden as rich vessels with wealth, deeds, spiritual exercises, virtues, and favors from God, never advancing because they lack the courage to make a complete break with some little satisfaction, attachment, or affection (which are all about the same), and thereby never reaching the port of perfection, which requires no more than a sudden flap of one's wings to tear the thread of attachment." "It makes little difference," he says, "whether a bird is tied by a thin thread or by a cord. Even if tied by a thread, the bird will be held bound just as surely as if it were tied by a cord."[70]

We must pray for the grace to see what cord or thread may be keeping us from allowing God to enter our poverty and put His love there. The rich young man was tied by the cord of many possessions. Although the religious sister we spoke of had renounced all her material possessions, it was the thin thread of the possibility

---

[70] St. John of the Cross, *The Ascent of Mount Carmel*, in *The Collected Works of St. John of the Cross*, bk. 1, chap. 11, pars. 4, 5.

of meeting Mr. Wonderful that held her bound. Both were given the grace to flap their wings "out of love for Him" and receive the one thing they were lacking, God as the person He is! Love!

Thankfully, when it comes to *Loving God,* the Lord is infinitely patient. If necessary, He literally has all eternity to love out of a soul all that is not of Him. He knows, as St. John of the Cross observes, that "all cannot be weaned at once."[71] "His Majesty," St. Teresa of Avila encourages, "knows well how to wait many days and years, especially when He sees perseverance and good desires." Regardless of how lukewarm our initial efforts in prayer are, "God esteems them highly," so do not "become disconsolate if you don't respond at once to the Lord."[72]

God is patient. "He knows well how to wait many days and years." He looked warmly upon my effort to get to Sunday Mass as a duty to check off to inherit eternal life. He lovingly beheld the Lent when it seemed a heroic effort to me as a young adult to commit to daily Mass for forty days. He smiled upon Fr. Bill Fahnlander as he regularly gave me the same, simple penance of looking at the crucifix while saying, "He did that for me" — knowing full well that when the truth of how "He did that for me" sank into my bones, the desire to carry out His command to "do this in memory of me" (Luke 22:19) would

---

[71] St. John of the Cross, *The Dark Night,* 1.9.9.
[72] St. Teresa of Avila, *The Interior Castle,* 2.1.3.

consume my soul and have me come to Him every day in Holy Mass, seeking the one thing I was lacking.

Each day at Mass the priest prays in the preparation of the altar and the offerings, "With humble spirit and contrite heart may we be accepted by you, O Lord, and may our sacrifice in your sight this day be pleasing to you, Lord God."

To be pleasing to the Bridegroom: that is the hope of His bride.

In the Second Eucharistic Prayer, we express our hope that "with the Blessed Virgin Mary, Mother of God, with blessed Joseph, her Spouse, with the blessed Apostles, and all the Saints who have pleased you throughout the ages, we may merit to be coheirs to eternal life."

What is most pleasing to God are the souls who receive Him as their Bridegroom. Souls who are intent on *Loving God* by allowing Him to sanctify them. *Loving God* by consenting to His work of creating in us a new, clean heart. *Loving God* by allowing Him to remove from our bodies the stony heart, and being made without spot or wrinkle or any such thing. *Loving God* as He loves out of us all that is not of Him, so that we, in turn, may come to "see him as he is" (1 John 3:2).

Open Wide the Doors for Christ!

In the inaugural homily of Benedict XVI, he reflected on the inaugural homily of St. Pope John Paul II, delivered in October 1978. He remarked on how these words of

John Paul II "constantly echo in my ears: 'Do not be afraid! Open wide the doors to Christ.'" Then, with his own penetrating words, Benedict XVI touches the depths of our souls by asking,

> Are we not perhaps all afraid in some way? If we let Christ enter fully into our lives, if we open ourselves totally to him, are we not afraid that He might take something away from us? Are we not perhaps afraid to give up something significant, something unique, something that makes life so beautiful? Do we not then risk ending up diminished and deprived of our freedom?[73]

To which the answer is given with resounding conviction,

> No! If we let Christ into our lives, we lose nothing, nothing, absolutely nothing of what makes life free, beautiful and great. Only in this friendship are the doors of life opened wide. Only in this friendship is the great potential of human existence truly revealed. Only in this friendship do we experience beauty and liberation.... He takes nothing away, and he gives you

---

[73] Benedict XVI, Homily for Mass, St. Peter's Square, April 24, 2005.

everything. When we give ourselves to him, we receive a hundredfold in return. Yes, open, open wide the doors to Christ — and you will find true life.[74]

Let us open wide the doors to Christ. Let us recognize Him as the Gift, the wonderful Bridegroom who has come to lay down His life for us, His bride. Let us strive to be the bride, with all that this means, allowing the Bridegroom to love out of us whatever is not of Him. To be full of love. For He asks nothing else, and we have nothing else to give.

[74] Ibid.

PART THREE

SERVING GOD

WHEN WE THINK of *Serving God*, the term "stewardship" will quite naturally come to mind. Some may be familiar with what is referred to as the "80/20 rule": how 80 percent of the time, talent, and treasure needed to keep a parish going is typically provided by 20 percent of the parishioners. In twenty-seven years of priestly ministry, I would say that is being generous. In practice, it can seem like 10 percent of the parishioners provide 90 percent of the time, talent, and treasure that is needed.

A pastor can spend a lot of time and energy trying to engage the other 90 percent. After two thousand years, you might think the Church would have stewardship down to a science, but *Serving God* is not a science. *Serving God* is what happens when we are *Knowing God* and *Loving God*, for then we will want to be where He is. As Jesus says, "Where I am, there also will my servant be" (John 12:26). *Serving God,* stewardship, is about being where Jesus is.

Stewardship is very, very important to Jesus. He tells us that the servant who is faithful in small matters will be entrusted with more. They will "share your master's joy" (Matt. 25:23). They will be where He is! The unfaithful steward, He relates in very sobering terms, will not be where He is. They will be cast out from His presence, "where there will be wailing and grinding of teeth" (Matt. 25:30). They will have missed out on their opportunity to be with Him.

Sparking a Desire to Serve

Realizing the utter importance of forming good stewards, our efforts to ignite some initial spark can be sentimental. We may bring in a dynamic speaker, provide a banquet with fine food, fill the evening with fun activities, give something away, maybe appeal to their sentiment of guilt. It might be a good first spark. And yet, to bear forth fruit that will last, it needs to be more than a spark.

Stewardship cannot be merely sentimental, for where Jesus is, we will not always want to be. "A sentiment can be a marvelous first spark," Benedict XVI reminded us earlier, "but it is not the fullness of love."[75] To be where Jesus is, to serve Him, will require us to grow in the fullness of love.

Peter, as we noted earlier, dropped everything to be with Jesus. Then Peter dropped the ball. We see in Peter how strong our sentiments can be. "Though all may have their faith in you shaken, mine will never be," Peter declared to Jesus. "Even though I should have to die with you, I will not deny you" (Matt. 26:33, 35). Sentiments, no matter how strong they may be, come and go. They are not an assurance that we will be where our Lord is.

---

[75] Benedict XVI, *Deus Caritas Est,* no. 17.

Peter's faith was shaken. He did not lay down his life. To avoid going where Jesus was, he denied even knowing Jesus three times. St. Teresa of Avila's warning rings true again: we "love ourselves very much."[76]

Our Lord's love for us, thankfully, is not sentimental. Jesus knew Peter, He loved Peter, and He beautifully returns from the dead to pursue Peter again.

A Call to Discipleship

Jesus knows that our attraction to Him is often a good, initial, sentimental spark. He also realizes that it is not yet the fullness of love. Even for those who drop everything to follow Jesus, there is a tendency to start looking again to get something for ourselves. "We have given up everything and followed you. What will there be for us?" (Matt. 19:27). Jesus knows that our love for the person He is will need to be disciplined and purified. He knows, as a wise monk observed, how the prospect of denying our self and picking up our cross daily "is not a very cheering one"; in fact, "the only attractive feature of the Cross is its relationship to Jesus."[77] Yet what a relationship that is! When we come to encounter God as the Mr. Wonderful He is, the Supreme Being, we will consider it a distinct privilege to be where He is, even when that is on the cross.

In time we come to appreciate how "no one else understands you as well he does, and no one knows like

---

[76] St. Teresa of Avila, *The Interior Castle*, 5.4.6.
[77] A Monk, *The Hermitage Within*, p. 79.

him how to console and help."[78] We will realize, along with St. Teresa, that we "couldn't find a better friend," that outside of this relationship "neither security nor peace will be found, that [we] should avoid going about to strange houses."[79] We will follow Him even when He leads us to where we do not want to go. For we will trust that He alone knows where we need to go to become more fully who God created us to be, where our own capacity to be filled by God will increase.

Without an authentic *Knowing of God* and *Loving of God,* "union with God — to our shame — is more attractive as the crowning of our own personality than as a disinterested response to his advances." There is a danger in losing "the sense of God in an exchange for an erroneous sense of man, by virtue of which man no longer presents himself as 'nothing' before the Godhead but as 'somebody' whom God has a duty to consider."[80]

Jesus Loves Us in Our Poverty

Through an authentic *Knowing of God,* we come to appreciate Him as He really is. God is Love; Jesus is Savior. The person God revealed Himself to be will always be where there is need of love, where there is need of being saved. In *Loving God,* we learned how "God needs nothing of our wealth, but He does need our poverty, through

---

[78] Ibid., p. 63.

[79] St. Teresa of Avila, *The Interior Castle,* 2.1.4.

[80] A Monk, *The Hermitage Within,* pp. 51–52.

which, alone, we may receive His gifts, His love, Himself. God is not able to be Himself, to be love, if He is not able to be self-outpouring into our hearts in the extravagant folly of His gratuitous love."[81]

The first place God leads us is to where *we* need to be loved, where *we* need to be saved. Our wounds, our sins, our weakness, our poverty, can sometimes prove to be the precise place we do not want to be led. Yet it is precisely there that we realize more deeply how we "couldn't find a better friend."[82] Jesus is the only Savior. God is the Love we need to be who He created us to be. He is the one thing we are lacking. By being with God in our poverty, where we need to be loved, where we need to be saved, we realize how "no one else understands you as well as he does, and no one knows like him how to console and help."[83]

God knew where Simon Peter needed to be led, to be who God created him to be. In this prospect of *Serving God*, there was no job description or need of a résumé. There was no sentimental appeal, not even to guilt. There was need for only one question: "Do you love me?" (John 21:16). Stewardship is not about "what we must do," to use the words of the rich young man. It is about not missing out on being where Jesus is, as the rich young man did. Jesus does not want Peter to miss out on

---

[81] A Carthusian, *The Way of Silent Love*, p. 28.
[82] St. Teresa of Avila, *The Interior Castle*, 2.1.4.
[83] A Monk, *The Hermitage Within*, p. 63.

being where He is, now and forever. He goes to where Peter needs to be loved, where Peter needs to be saved. Three times Peter had denied even knowing who Jesus was, so three times Jesus asks Peter, "Do you love me?"

The first time Jesus asked, "Do you love me," he used the Greek word *agape*. Peter responded, "Yes Lord, you know that I love you," using the Greek word *phileo*. Jesus asked Peter again, "Do you love me," still using the Greek word *agape*. Peter again responded, "Yes, Lord, you know that I love you," using the word *phileo*.

This exchange has been interpreted in several ways. In this context it seems fair to suggest that perhaps Peter remained aware that he had not loved Jesus in a sacrificial way. How could he respond *agape,* when he did not lay down his life for Jesus? What is telling, then, is how Jesus meets Peter where he is. Jesus knows Peter, Jesus loves Peter.

So the third time Jesus asks Peter, "Do you love me," He uses *phileo*. He then goes on to reveal how Peter will be led to love Jesus in a sacrificial *agape* manner: " 'When you were younger, you used to dress yourself and go where you wanted; but when you grow old, you will stretch out your hands, and someone else will dress you and lead you where you do not want to go.' He said this signifying by what kind of death he would glorify God. And when he had said this, he said to him, 'Follow me' " (John 21:18–19). Jesus knew where Simon Peter needed to be led to become the saint he was created to be.

Jesus Loves Us to Holiness

Just as Jesus met Peter where he needed to be loved, where he needed to be saved, He does the same thing for each of us. We can see this clearly in the lives of the saints.

Jesus knew where Agnes Gonxha Bojaxhiu needed to be led, to be who God created her to be. Mother Teresa wasn't looking for opportunities to do something hard with her life. She was a soul who loved the Lord and strongly desired to be where He is. Our Lord led her to be with Him, in what she would come to recognize as "Jesus, in the distressing disguise of the poorest of the poor." It was there that she would be who God created her to be, where her own capacity to be filled by God would increase.

An American tourist in India stood by in awe as he watched Mother Teresa lovingly clean the infected wounds of a horribly disfigured leper. "Sister," he commented, "I wouldn't do that for a million dollars!" Her response: "Neither would I, brother. Neither would I do what I do for a million dollars. But for the love of God, I do it gladly."

We are grateful Mother Teresa did not miss out on being where Jesus is, even in the distressing disguise of the poorest of the poor—especially in the distressing disguise of the poorest of the poor. Our Lord knew where Agnes Gonxha Bojaxhiu needed to be led to become St. Teresa of Calcutta. In her we see the fulfillment of St. Catherine of Siena's observation, "Be who God meant you to be, and you will set the world on fire."

Our Lord knew where Karol Wojtyla needed to be led, to be who God created him to be, where his own capacity to be filled by God would increase. In the homily of his Mass of Thanksgiving on the twenty-fifth anniversary of his pontificate, he reflected how "at the Conclave, through the College of Cardinals, Christ said to me, as He once said to Peter by the Lake of Gennesaret, 'Tend my sheep.' I heard echo in my soul the question He addressed to Peter at that moment, 'Do you love me? Do you love me more than these?'" After detailing his acceptance, he went on to confide how "every day that same dialogue between Jesus and Peter takes place in my heart. In spirit, I focus on the benevolent gaze of the risen Christ. Although He knows of my human frailty, He encourages me to answer confidently, like Peter, 'Lord, you know everything; you know that I love you.' And then He invites me to take on the responsibility that He Himself has entrusted to me."[84] Our Lord knew where Karol Wojtyla needed to be led to become St. John Paul II.

It is by being alone with God in our heart that we will hear Our Lord ask, "Do you love me?" If we listen carefully, we will hear Him ask us again and again and again. We must pray for the desire to truly know Him,

---

[84] St. John Paul II, *Homily at Mass of Thanksgiving on the 25th Anniversary of the Pontificate*, St. Peter's Square, October 16, 2003.

love Him, and be where He is. One thing we cannot give to another human being is desire. We might tell another person why they might want to be where the Lord is. We can strive to model for others what it might look like to be where the Lord is. But we cannot give to another person the desire to be where the Lord is. It is they who must be pierced by the Lord asking them, "Do you love me?" It is they who must desire to be where He is.

A Carthusian observes,

> One of the most beautiful definitions of a monk is that he is a man of desire.... The day when he feels full to overflowing, he ceases to be a monk—and is living an illusion. God never surfeits us with the gift of himself but creates in us an ever larger capacity for love and, having done this, he replenishes us with a desire, a thirst, more ardent still. And it will always be this way with God for eternity without end, because God is without end. If we arrive at the end, it is not God.[85]

A Promise to Serve

A significant moment for a priest in the Rite of Ordination involves the placing of his hands inside the hands of the

---

[85] A Carthusian, *The Way of Silent Love*, p. 28.

ordaining bishop, promising respect and obedience to him and his successors. It is so significant, we do it twice: at our ordination as a transitional deacon and again as a priest.

When I was about to be ordained a transitional deacon in Rome, I was wrestling with this promise of obedience. I was still discerning whether God might be calling me to a contemplative vocation. In the years leading up to my ordination as a transitional deacon, I had visited several religious contemplative communities. At the time, our diocese did not have a bishop. Bishop Kinney had been moved to the Diocese of St. Cloud and Bishop Zipfel was not yet named as our ordinary. So I was not able to talk this over with my bishop while at home over the summer months.

When I returned to Rome just months prior to my ordination, my spiritual director was away, so I could not talk it over with him either. God then led me to go and pray at the convent chapel of the sisters who ran the homeless shelter where I had regularly volunteered while in the seminary. The person He had waiting there to help me work out this dilemma was their humble superior.

Was God calling me to serve Him as a diocesan priest or a contemplative monk? As I listed off the gifts I felt I had to serve in either capacity, this holy nun soberly cut through it all with one simple question, "Do you think God needs your gifts and talents to save the world?"

I didn't respond, stunned by the question. I evidently did think He was needing to use the gifts I had. She continued, "He doesn't! He needs *you*! Give yourself to Him and let Him decide how to use you!" In a single breath, this wise soul cut through twenty-seven years of worldly formation. She knew that in the end *Serving God* is not about the actual work that we do. It is about *Knowing God, Loving God,* and desiring to be where He is. Our Lord knows where I need to be, to become more fully who I am, where my own capacity to be filled by God will increase. In the words of St. Teresa of Avila, "There was no need for me to be advising Him."[86]

I did go on to make my promise of obedience in Rome as a transitional deacon. Then I made that promise again in Bismarck when Bishop Zipfel ordained me a priest.

The first thing Bishop Zipfel asked of me out of obedience was to be a high school instructor. I responded by informing him that was the last thing I wanted to do. He then informed me that he wasn't asking me, he was telling me. With that, I was assigned as parochial vicar at Our Lady of Grace in Minot and part-time high school instructor at Bishop Ryan High School. After only one year there, I was sent to the Cathedral of the Holy Spirit in Bismarck and taught at St. Mary's Central High School. Two years later, I received my first assignment as a pastor at Queen of the Most Holy Rosary in Stanley.

[86] St. Teresa of Avila, *The Interior Castle*, 2.1.8.

On my first official day as pastor, we broke ground on building a new church. After six grace-filled years in this parish and nine years of dialogue with Bishop Zipfel over the possibility of living a more contemplative vocation, I was given permission to live one year as a diocesan hermit, as a time for us both to make a proper discernment. Three years later, I made a promise to live as a diocesan hermit for the rest of my life.

And then, after six years as a hermit, my health hit a roadblock.

Complications after a few surgeries made it difficult for me to carry out the manual labor needed to live in the hermitage. With the winter months approaching, I was able to go and recuperate in the parish of a priest-friend of mine in Tampa, Florida. While I was away, Bishop Zipfel retired and Bishop Kagan was ordained.

When I returned in the spring, I came to St. Anne's in Bismarck with the intention of continuing to heal and return to the hermitage. However, while I was in residence at St. Anne's, the pastor retired, and I was asked to remain on as pastor, which I did for the next ten years. During the last few years of that assignment, Bishop Kagan and I discerned the possibility of a return to something more contemplative. Presently I am around a year into a new role as the diocesan spiritual director.

The advice I was given by that wise, holy nun over twenty-eight years ago was well received, and now it has been deeply learned. "Give yourself to God and let Him decide how to use you." Looking back, I can appreciate how it has been a process of learning how *Serving God* is not about the actual work that we do; it is about *Knowing God, Loving God,* and desiring to be where He is. It is about trusting that He knows where I need to be led to be who I am created to be, where my own capacity to be filled by God would increase.

Mother Teresa would counsel her sisters, "We are at Jesus' disposal. If He wants you sick in bed, if He wants you to proclaim His work in the street, if He wants you to clean the toilets all day, that's all right, everything is all right. We must say, 'I belong to you. You can do whatever you like.' And this is our strength, and this is the joy of the Lord."

Mother Teresa knew that in the end, *Serving God* is not about the actual work that we do. It is about *Knowing God, Loving God*, and desiring to be where He is.

When We Don't Want to Go

You might imagine how much of a whiplash it was for me, to go from living as a hermit for six years to being the pastor of one of the largest parishes in the diocese. Those first months as pastor were crazy, and it would be some time before they settled down.

A few months into this new assignment, I scheduled a few days of retreat up at the hermitage. Surprisingly, after only one beautiful day back in the hermitage, I felt a strong sense that I needed to return to the parish. I ignored this impulse, telling the Lord that I still had a few more days at the hermitage. So I stayed, and the Lord went back to the parish.

In a very short time, I realized how much grace God had given me to live for those six years as a hermit. My cell very quickly went from being a *caelum,* a heaven, to being a mere *cella,* a cell I was stuck in all by myself. After only one day I couldn't take it anymore and went back to the parish. I needed to be where He was.

There is a story of Peter being led where he did not want to go. When it became evident that they were looking to crucify him, Peter fled Rome. Along the road outside the city, he meets the Risen Lord.

Peter asks Jesus, "Where are you going?" (In Latin, the memorable *Quo Vadis?*)

Jesus replies, "I am going to Rome to be crucified again."

So Peter turns around and returns to Rome, having regained the courage to be where the Lord is. There Peter is martyred by being crucified upside down. The "kind of death [by which] he would glorify God" (John 21:19). The unique manner by which we most fully know Peter as he was created to be, where his capacity to be filled by God was increased.

Clay in the Potter's Hands

In a book entitled *The Freedom of Obedience,* a Carthusian novice master helps us to recognize, "To reach the Creator

… I must smash all the molds in which I continually shape myself, because they are always limited; I must reject all security, familiar words, riches, offer myself utterly poor, virgin, to the breath of the Spirit."[87]

All these molds in which we continually shape ourselves, in which we strive to find security, must be smashed. We must strive to be "like clay in the hand of the potter" (Jer. 18:6), recognizing how the potter has "a right over the clay" (Rom. 9:21). For outside of this potter's house, "neither security nor peace will be found."[88] To be who God created us to be, for our capacity to be filled by Him to continually increase, we must be willing to be formed by Him again and again in matters big and in matters small.

On a recent vacation with my dad and his wife to the North Shore of Minnesota, we planned a day trip to Grand Marais, known for its art galleries featuring the many local artists. Along the way, there was so much natural beauty to enjoy that by the time we arrived in Grand Marais, the art galleries were just closing. I had been hoping to enjoy some of the paintings of the beautiful scenery we were enjoying and to purchase a coffee mug made by a local potter. But just as we arrived at 4:55, we found the galleries in Grand Marias closing precisely at 5:00 p.m.

How easy it would have been to remain stuck in the mold I had envisaged for that evening, wailing and

---

[87] A Carthusian, *The Freedom of Obedience* (London: Darton, Longman and Todd, 1998), p. 27.

[88] St. Teresa of Avila, *The Interior Castle,* 2.1.4.

grinding my teeth outside the locked doors of art galleries! With the galleries closed, we arrived back to the cabin we were renting just in time for a stunning sunset. We stayed out on the shores of Lake Superior for over an hour, watching the brilliant colors dance over and through the sky and lake. How good God was to close the art galleries in Grand Marais, so that we might enjoy His hand at work in unmatched artistry. When you are on the shores of Lake Superior enjoying the sunset, you are not missing paintings of sunsets on Lake Superior.

As I was making my own way back up to the cabin for Evening Prayer, thanking the Lord for that lesson, I managed to quip, "Now how about the pottery?" The reply came clearly, "I am the potter, you are the clay." Timely words to hear, being only a few months out of having the mold of a pastor smashed and being shaped into a new role as the diocesan spiritual director. God was using this small matter to further mold me in the trust needed to be freely formed into who He created me to be, where my capacity to be filled by God will increase, where I will come to know Him more deeply as Love, as Savior.

In matters big and small, we are being molded into trusting that the Lord "knows what He is about." Those are the closing words of a beautiful, telling meditation written by St. John Henry Newman. His prayer reflects a soul who has come to appreciate how, in the end, *Serving God* is not about the actual work that we do. It is about *Knowing God, Loving God*, and desiring to be where He is.

We are all created to His glory—we are created to do His will. I am created to do something or to be something for which no one else is created; I have a place in God's counsels, in God's world, which no one else has; whether I be rich or poor, despised or esteemed by man, God knows me and calls me by my name.

God has created me to do Him some definite service; He has committed some work to me which He has not committed to another. I have my mission—I never may know it in this life, but I shall be told it in the next. Somehow I am necessary for His purposes, as necessary in my place as an Archangel in his—if, indeed, I fail, He can raise another, as He would make the stones children of Abraham. Yet I have a part in this great work; I am a link in a chain, a bond of connection between persons. He has not created me for naught. I shall do good; I shall do His work; I shall be an angel of peace, a preacher of truth in my own place, while not intending it, if I do but keep His commandments and serve Him in my calling.

> *Therefore, I will trust Him, whatever I am,*
> *I can never be thrown away. If I am in*
> *sickness, my sickness may serve Him; in*
> *perplexity, my perplexity may serve Him; If*
> *I am in sorrow, my sorrow may serve Him.*
> *My sickness, or perplexity, or sorrow may be*
> *necessary causes of some great end, which is*
> *quite beyond us. He does nothing in vain;*
> *He may prolong my life, He may shorten it;*
> *He knows what He is about. He may take*
> *away my friends, He may throw me among*
> *strangers, He may make me feel desolate,*
> *make my spirits sink, hide my future from*
> *me—still, He knows what He is about.*[89]

"He knows what He is about." "He does nothing in vain." These are important truths to be molded in. For "sometimes," St. Teresa of Avila warns, "the devil gives us great desires so that we will avoid setting ourselves to the task at hand, serving Our Lord in possible things, and instead be content with having desired the impossible." When it comes to *Serving God,* "We shouldn't build castles in the air."[90]

---

[89] St. John Henry Newman, "Hope in God — Creator," March 7, 1848, in *Meditations and Devotions,* part 3, Meditations on Christian Doctrine, ed. Rev. W. P. Neville, at Newman Reader, National Institute for Newman Studies, https://newmanreader .org/works/meditations/meditations9.html#doctrine1.

[90] St. Teresa of Avila, *The Interior Castle,* 7.4.14, 15.

There were no castles being built in the air by St. John Henry Newman. He knew, as did St. Teresa, that in *Serving God*, "the Lord doesn't look so much at the greatness of our works as at the love with which they are done."[91] A wisdom St. Teresa of Calcutta came to echo in spelling out how

> To the Almighty God the smallest action given to Him is great.... What should be important for us is how much love we put into giving ... fidelity to small things with great love—the smaller the thing, the greater the love.... What is really important is that we really become holy—that tender love, that fidelity to small things with great love. Little Flower was canonized because she did small things with extraordinary love.[92]

Our Lord Himself warns that

> not everyone who says to me, "Lord, Lord," will enter the kingdom of heaven, but only the one who does the will of my Father in heaven. Many will say to me on that day, "Lord, Lord, did we not prophesy

---

91 Ibid., 7.4.15.
92 St. Teresa of Calcutta, *Where There Is Love, There Is God,* comp. and ed. Brian Koldodiejchuk, M.C. (New York: Doubleday Religion, 2010), pp. 324–325.

> in your name? Did we not drive out de-
> mons in your name? Did we not do mighty
> deeds in your name?" Then I will declare to
> them solemnly, "I never knew you. Depart
> from me, you evildoers." (Matt. 7:21–23)

Serving God is not about the actual work that we do, not even the work of prophesying in God's name, driving out demons in His name, or doing mighty deeds in His name. In the end, it truly is about *Knowing God, Loving God,* and being where He is.

Let the Glory of God Fill You

In the work God has committed to me, I have learned the importance of asking myself two key questions:

1. Why am I doing what I am doing?

2. Who am I doing it for?

If the answer is anything other than "for the Lord and His glory," I have the wrong answer. It is God who gives the greatness to our work, leading us to possible things. Leading us to where we will come to know Him, love Him, and be with Him, now and forever. The *Baltimore Catechism* was good to instill in us that union with God is a possible thing: "God made us to show forth His goodness and to share with us His everlasting happiness in heaven."

It is by *Knowing God, Loving God,* and *Serving God* in this world that we allow the Lord "to share with us His goodness." The time we have in this world will determine our capacity for enjoying "His everlasting happiness of heaven." When it dawned on St. Thérèse of Lisieux that there will be different capacities for being filled by God in Heaven, she "was surprised that God didn't give equal glory to all the Elect in heaven and was afraid all would not be perfectly happy."[93]

To help console Thérèse, her sister Pauline had her fetch a tiny sewing thimble and their father's large drinking tumbler to fill both to the brim with water. After filling them both to their capacity, she asked Thérèse which was fuller. Thérèse was then able to see how "each was as full as the other and it was impossible to put in more water than they could contain." Pauline had helped Thérèse "to understand that in heaven God will grant His Elect as much glory as they can take, the last having nothing to envy in the first."[94] I often reflect with others on how in Heaven we will get a new body, but the soul we die with is ours forever. This brief time on earth is given to determine the capacity of our soul forever. That is why God is so intent upon leading us to where our capacity to be filled by Him will increase.

Finding Peace Within

There is a prayer attributed to Thérèse, which some also attribute to St. Teresa of Avila, while still others claim a

---

[93] St. Thérèse of Lisieux, *Story of a Soul*, 3rd ed., trans. John Clarke, O.C.D. (Washington, D.C.: ICS Publications, 1996), pp. 44–45.

[94] Ibid., p. 45.

more modern author. Perhaps this makes it all the more a prayer we can simply receive for the truth to which it leads us without considering its source. It is a beautiful encouragement for those striving to trust God in leading them to where they are meant to be, to where our capacity to be filled by Him can increase.

> *May today there be peace within.*
>
> *May you trust God that you are*
> *exactly where you are meant to be.*
>
> *May you not forget the infinite*
> *possibilities that are born of faith.*
>
> *May you use those gifts that you have*
> *received and pass on the love that has*
> *been given to you. May you be content*
> *knowing you are a child of God.*
>
> *Let this presence settle into your bones*
> *and allow your soul the freedom to*
> *sing, dance, praise and love. It is*
> *there for each and every one of us.*[95]

"May today there be peace within." God's plan for this "peace within" had remained an idea for thousands of years.

---

[95] The origin of this prayer is not clear. Some accredit it to St. Thérèse of Lisieux, others to St. Teresa of Avila, and still others to Minnie Louise Haskins, who published it in a book of poems titled *The Desert* in 1908.

St. Bernard of Clairvaux was reflecting on the book of the Prophet Jeremiah, where the Lord had revealed how He was thinking "thoughts of peace and not affliction" (Jer. 29:11). "Yet," St. Bernard observed, "your thought was locked within you, and whatever you thought, we did not know, for who knew the mind of the Lord, or who was his counselor? And so," he continues, "the idea of peace came down to do the work of peace: *The Word was made flesh* and even now *dwells among us.*"[96]

What a joy it is for us to know now how the Word, which was in the beginning thinking thoughts of peace, thoughts which we did not know, "became flesh and made His dwelling among us" (John 1:14). How eager the apostle John was to share how "what was from the beginning, what we have heard, what we have seen with our eyes, what we looked upon and touched with our hands … we proclaim now to you, so that you may have fellowship with us; for our fellowship is with the Father and with His Son, Jesus Christ" (1 John 1:1–3). God's plan for peace on earth is no longer an idea. It is a Person! A Person who has come and will come again! "May today there be peace within."

On the tenth anniversary of my ordination as a priest, I went on pilgrimage to Jerusalem. Unfortunately, like today, it was not a peaceful place. Gunshots could be

---

[96] From a sermon by St. Bernard of Clairvaux, as found in *The Liturgy of Hours,* vol. 4 (New York: Catholic Book Publishing Co., 1975), p. 1471. The words from the book of Jeremiah are as quoted by St. Bernard.

heard and, at one time, even a bomb. There were military checkpoints between the various quarters.

It might sound like the beginning of a bad joke, but while I was in the Holy City with three other priests, we encountered a local rabbi at Ben & Jerry's. ("Four priests and a rabbi meet up at a Ben & Jerry's in Jerusalem....") But it was no joke—and became even less funny when the rabbi decided to confront us. "Do you really believe Jesus was the Messiah? If the Messiah had come, there would be peace on earth, peace in Jerusalem."

It was quite jarring. I grew up in North Dakota and can't recall ever being challenged in that manner. We responded that the Messiah has come, and that the peace He gives is not given in the way that the world gives peace. The peace He came to bring is our reconciliation with the Father. The rabbi retorted that if this were so, a kingdom of peace would be established. We replied that Jesus has restored us to the Kingdom of Heaven. The rabbi was silent, and a concerted look of disdain and disbelief came over him. He firmly stated, "You are here, where Jesus came. You see all this fighting here. When the Messiah comes, will not every tear be wiped away?"

"That will happen when He comes again," we reassured him.

He smirked and quipped, "When He comes again, we will ask Him if He was here before."

God's plan for peace on earth remained an idea to this rabbi. For him God was merely thinking thoughts of peace, thoughts that were inaccessible to him. Today, there was for him no "peace within." When we think of peace in a worldly way, like this rabbi in Jerusalem, we think of harmony. The word Jesus used for peace in Hebrew is *shalom*. *Shalom* is used to convey a harmony, yet its deeper meaning is a wholeness, a completeness.

Prior to His death, Jesus prepared His disciples for this deeper meaning by explaining, "Peace I leave with you; my peace I give to you. Not as the world gives do I give it to you. Do not let your hearts be troubled or afraid" (John 14:27). The peace Jesus would return from the grave to give His disciples is the completeness, the wholeness of salvation. By dying He would destroy our death, and by rising He would restore our life. Jesus would complete the Paschal Mystery.

The disciples of Jesus, like this rabbi in Jerusalem, "were hoping that he would be the one to redeem Israel" (Luke 24:21), to restore harmony to their nation. When Jesus and His disciples entered Jerusalem, the capital city, people enthusiastically spread their cloaks on the road before Jesus to ride over while they triumphantly proclaimed, "Blessed is the king who comes in the name of the Lord. Peace in heaven and glory in the highest" (Luke 19:36–38). The peace, the harmony they were hoping for was quickly disrupted, for in just a few days "our chief priests and rulers both handed him over to a sentence of death and crucified him" (Luke 24:20). Their greatest fears had unfolded before their very eyes. Then, "for fear of the Jews" (John 20:19), the disciples of Jesus locked themselves behind closed doors.

Putting Your Fears in Order

I recently heard of a man who was receiving an award for his courage in speaking out on controversial issues. He began his acceptance speech by remarking that "people will say to me that I have courage. That's not right. That's not true. I have my fears in order." He was so close to getting something so beautifully right. He was correct in acknowledging that we all have fears. He was also correct in the need to have our fears in order. What he unfortunately missed is that having our fears in order is precisely what the virtue of courage is.

Prior to His death, Jesus also prepared His disciples to put their fears in order, as He foretold, "In the world you will have trouble, but take courage, I have conquered the world" (John 16:33). In the First Eucharistic Prayer we pray for God to "order our days in your peace." The fears of Jesus' disciples were put in order as He suddenly stood with them, behind those locked doors, to proclaim, "Peace be with you" (John 20:21).

He needed to say it three times, for outside those doors there was no harmony. For there to be "peace within" these disciples, they would need to *know* the

Risen Lord, *love* the Risen Lord, and venture outside those locked doors to be where the Risen Lord is, "to go to Galilee, and there they will see me" (Matt. 28:10). From Galilee they would be sent to *serve* the Risen Lord "like sheep in the midst of wolves," people would "hand [them] over to courts and scourge [them] in their synagogues," and they would "be led before governors and kings for my sake as a witness before them and the pagans." They would "be hated by all because of my name" (Matt. 10:16–18, 22).

Imagine the fear this must have raised in their hearts when Our Lord prepared them for this prior to His death. Those fears were now put in order. There was "peace within," when they came to *know* the Risen Lord, *love* the Risen Lord, and *serve* the Risen Lord by allowing Him to lead them to where they would be who God created them to be, where their own capacity to be filled by God would increase.

Within every Mass the priest extends this very telling greeting, "The peace of the Lord be with you." To which the reply is given, "And with your spirit." This exchange is no mere dialogue of ideas. It is the shared relationship we have with a Person, the Person who is our peace, who has made our peace "by the blood of his cross" (Col. 1:20). Those who share in this authentic relationship realize, as did Benedict XVI, how "the peace of Christ is not synonymous with the mere absence of conflicts. On the contrary, Jesus' peace is the result of a constant battle against evil."[97]

At every Mass, we celebrate that the battle against evil has been won. The dismissal of Mass is a fitting way to conclude our time reflecting on *Knowing God, Loving God,* and *Serving God.* The Latin dismissal of Mass is "*Ite missa est*": literally translated, "Go, it is sent." Not *you* are sent, but *it* is sent. *It* is the relationship we enjoy as a bride with the Bridegroom. *Sent,* as if on a mission.

Sent off from enjoying these "sacred mysteries" that transcend time and space, with the mission of bringing the love of that relationship into the times and spaces our Bridegroom sends us. Sent off to do possible things in predictable places, like our families and our places of work. Sent off to do possible things in unpredictable places, like the least of our brethren and our enemies. Sent off to be the "instruments of peace" that St. Francis of Assisi prayed we might be. "Not a peace that is inconsistent and only apparent," as Benedict XVI reflected on this prayer, "but one that is real, pursued with courage and tenacity in the daily commitment to overcome evil with good and paying in the person the price that this entails."[98]

Mother Teresa would pray this same Prayer for Peace with her sisters every day immediately after Mass, before they went out for their mission. (For your convenience, it

---

[97] Benedict XVI, Angelus, August 19, 2007.
[98] Ibid.

is provided as the conclusion to this book.) I have found it helpful to pray this prayer two times through. The first time with an openness of heart to receive these gifts from God. That where there is hatred in me, I might receive His love; where there is darkness in me, I might receive His light. I first need to receive these gifts of peace from God. Then, to pray it a second time through with the hope of being an instrument of the very gifts we receive from Him. In other words, where there are not these gifts of His peace in me, may God put them, so that these same gifts of peace may then be drawn out of me.

"May today there be peace within." With our fears in order, let us realize our mission to share with others the God we know, the God we love, the God we serve, the God who is our peace. As an English variation of the dismissal of Mass sends us forth, may we now "Go in peace."

Lord, make me an instrument of Your peace;
where there is hatred, I may bring love;
where there is injury, I may bring the
spirit of forgiveness;
that where there is discord, I may bring
harmony;
where there is error, I may bring truth;
where there is doubt, I may bring faith;
where there is despair, I may bring hope;
where there are shadows, I may bring light;
where there is sadness, I may bring joy.

Lord, grant that I may seek rather to
comfort than to be comforted;
to understand than to be understood;
to love than to be loved;
for it is by self-forgetting that one finds,
it is by forgiving that one is forgiven,
it is by dying that one is born to eternal life.

Amen[99]

---

[99] Prayer for Peace. Though commonly associated with St. Francis of Assisi, who lived in the thirteenth century, modern research has challenged this, contending that the author is not known.

BIBLIOGRAPHY

A Carthusian. *The Way of Silent Love*. London: Darton, Longman and Todd, 1994.

A Carthusian. *The Freedom of Obedience*. London: Darton, Longman and Todd, 1998.

A Monk. *The Hermitage Within: Spirituality of the Desert*. London: Darton, Longman and Todd, 1999.

Benedict XVI (Ratzinger, Joseph Cardinal). *A New Song for the Lord: Faith in Christ and Liturgy Today*. New York: Crossroad, 1996.

Benedict XVI. Angelus. August 19, 2007.

Benedict XVI. Encyclical Letter *Deus Caritas Est*: God Is Love. December 25, 2005.

Benedict XVI. *God and the World: A Conversation with Peter Seewald*. San Francisco: Ignatius Press, 2002.

Benedict XVI. Homily for Mass for the Beginning of the Petrine Ministry of the Bishop of Rome. St. Peter's Square. April 24, 2005.

Benedict XVI. Post-Synodal Apostolic Exhortation *Sacramentum Caritatis*: The Sacrament of Charity. February 22, 2007.

Bernard of Clairvaux, St. *The Liturgy of Hours*. Vol. 4. New York: Catholic Book Publishing Co., 1975.

Bernard of Clairvaux, St. *On the Song of Songs*. Vol. 4. Translated by Irene Edmonds. Kalamazoo, MI: Cistercian Publications, 1980.

Catechism of the Catholic Church. St. Paul, MN: The Wanderer Press, 1994.

Chapman, Gary. *The 5 Love Languages: The Secret to Love That Lasts*. Chicago: Northfield Publishing, 2015.

Cloud of Unknowing, The. Garden City, NY: Image Books, 1973.

John of the Cross, St. *The Collected Works of St. John of the Cross*. Translated by Kieran Kavanaugh, O.C.D., and Otilio Rodriguez, O.C.D. Washington DC: Institute of Carmelite Studies, 1973.

John Paul II, St. Homily at Mass of Thanksgiving on the 25th Anniversary of the Pontificate. St. Peter's Square. October 16, 2003.

Lewis, C.S. (Clive Staples). *The Four Loves*. New York: HarperCollins, 1960.

The Navarre Bible: St. John. Dublin: Four Courts Press, 1997.

Newman, St. John Henry. "Hope in God—Creator," March 7, 1848. In *Meditations and Devotions*. Part 3, Meditations on Christian Doctrine. Edited by Rev. W. P. Neville. At Newman Reader, National Institute for Newman Studies. https://newmanreader.org/works/ meditations/meditations9.html#doctrine1.

Pieper, Joseph. *Faith—Hope—Love*. San Francisco: Ignatius Press, 1997.

Teresa of Calcutta, St. *Come Be My Light.* New York: Doubleday, 2007.

Teresa of Calcutta, St. *Where There Is Love, There Is God.* Compiled and edited by Brian Koldodiejchuk, M.C. New York: Doubleday Religion, 2010.

Teresa of Avila, St. *The Collected Works of St. Teresa of Avila,* 3 vols. Translated by Kieran Kavanaugh, O.C.D., and Otilio Rodriguez, O.C.D. Washington DC: Institute of Carmelite Studies, 1987.

Thérèse of Lisieux, St. *Story of a Soul.* 3rd ed. Translated by John Clarke, O.C.D. Washington, DC: ICS Publications, 1996.

Thérèse of Lisieux, St. *Her Last Conversations.* Translated by John Clarke, O.C.D. Washington, DC: ICS Publications, 1977.

Ward, Benedicta. *The Sayings of the Desert Fathers.* Kalamazoo, MI: Cistercian Publications, 1984.

William of St. Thierry. *The Golden Epistle.* Translated by Theodore Berkeley, O.C.S.O. Kalamazoo, MI: Cistercian Publications, 1980.

AUTHOR BIOGRAPHY

Fr. Wayne Sattler has been a priest of the Diocese of Bismarck since 1997. He was an instructor in two diocesan high schools for three years, served as a pastor for sixteen years, and lived a life of prayerful solitude as a diocesan hermit for six years. During that time, as a fruit of this call as a hermit, Fr. Sattler gave retreats to priests and religious, particularly the Missionaries of Charity. In 2023, he began a new role as diocesan spiritual director for the Bismarck Diocese. In this role, along with providing spiritual direction, he has given numerous retreats, talks, and parish missions. He is the author of the book *And You Will Find Rest: What God Does in Prayer*, which is used as a text for a class he teaches annually at the University of Mary as well as in the permanent diaconate formation program in his diocese.

Sophia Institute

Sophia Institute is a nonprofit institution that seeks to nurture the spiritual, moral, and cultural life of souls and to spread the gospel of Christ in conformity with the authentic teachings of the Roman Catholic Church.

Sophia Institute Press fulfills this mission by offering translations, reprints, and new publications that afford readers a rich source of the enduring wisdom of mankind.

Sophia Institute also operates the popular online resource CatholicExchange.com. *Catholic Exchange* provides world news from a Catholic perspective as well as daily devotionals and articles that will help readers to grow in holiness and live a life consistent with the teachings of the Church.

In 2013, Sophia Institute launched Sophia Teachers to renew and rebuild Catholic culture through service to Catholic education. With the goal of nurturing the spiritual, moral, and cultural life of souls, and an abiding respect for the role and work of teachers, we strive to provide materials and programs that are at once enlightening to the mind and ennobling to the heart; faithful and complete, as well as useful and practical.

Sophia Institute gratefully recognizes the Solidarity Association for preserving and encouraging the growth of our apostolate over the course of many years. Without their generous and timely support, this book would not be in your hands.

www.SophiaInstitute.com
www.CatholicExchange.com
www.SophiaTeachers.org